A MOMENT OF GRACE

A Retrospective of Ed Fraga
1981 - 2001

MEADOW BROOK ART GALLERY
October 12 - November 12, 2001

Curated by Dick Goody

with an essay by
MaryAnn Wilkinson
Curator of Modern and Contemporary Art
The Detroit Institute of Arts

This exhibition and catalogue was made possible by a generous gift from
Annette Balian

ED FRAGA

Recently, in the west, the disposition of humanity, and inquiries into the nature of existence, have become fatigued and undermined by frustration, anxiety and uncertainty. It is not that the nature of being is obscured by the deliberate chaos of materialism; rather materialism has veiled the ephemeral vulnerability of humanity. The mortal realm has obscured that of the spirit. Over the last fifty years, contemporary art, particularly in America, has incessantly and inexorably revealed the apex and debasement of the material realm. It has been an avid excursion and such exposure has not always been ironic; indeed, much of it demonstrates the glee of arch contentment. The temple of materialism is both extrovert and gushing.

How extraordinary then to encounter a quiet room of paintings which explore the introverted realm of the self. The paintings of Ed Fraga whisper; they urge us to slow down and breath slowly. The feeling is not unlike an intimate, ambulatory progress around a medieval cathedral. The process of looking at Fraga's work requires a shift in perception as if one is compelled to adopt an unhurried, deliberate, reflective mode being. Quite clearly these paintings allude to instances of being, or at least to the curious space between being and its antithesis. It is a contemplative arena, though *arena* implies publicity and the space in Fraga's work, though often vast in scale, psychologically is intimate and introverted. Each encounter with his work is a private encounter tempered by one's own subconscious. It is a compelling task to attempt to identify the specific temporal allusions, but since the images are neither material nor ethereal such an endeavor is ultimately doomed to fail. This might suggest that they disguise the lacuna between being and its cessation, but instead of believing that such a place exists, it is perhaps more suitable to consider that Fraga's dramas occupy a deeper subconscious, subliminal realm.

These are not whimsical fantasies, neither are they overtly evangelically religious. Fraga's subconscious scenarios are modified and shaped by a potent urban manifestation. Often Fraga's images employ inner-city architectural devices; this evokes something of the cult of *the Detroit artist* in the work – that powerful evocation of decayed industrial materialism. This gritty presentation prevents the work from becoming wistful and irrational. Architecture has not been a prescribed component in Western painting since Caravaggio all but banished it with his dynamic reinterpretation of the figure at the beginning of the seventeenth century. Prior to this, the architectonic fifteenth & sixteenth century anconas of Italy, and polytychs of Belgium, served to place miraculous images of saints and angels in a firmly accessible terrestrial context. The massive ornamental gold leafed frames imitated the architectural surroundings bringing the viewer down to earth. The architectural manifestation in Fraga's paintings achieves a similar purpose and provides another connection between the artist and the quattrocento.

Fraga evokes individual fallibility by making human images that are the complete reverse of stereotypic perfection, that is to say that if such perfection is embodied by the gregarious beauties of chic television commercials, Fraga's models are inward-looking, eccentric and the inversion of tall, tan and self confident. Not exactly flawed, they are imprisoned in furtive bodies by an overwhelming sense of culpability; its source is less overt than guilt, it is a sort of defeatist resignation born of intrinsic original sin. The artist is clearly concerned with consequences. Again, this preoccupation with cause and effect presents a powerful connection with fifteenth century Flemish painting which resoundingly informs us that bad things will happen to bad people.

Intellectually, Fraga knows that to seduce the viewer is to cast his spell. The incantation is masterfully achieved through perfect technique. Realism is no longer blacklisted, but in 1979 when he started painting, the prospects for a figurative painter were not particularly encouraging. Shrewdly, Fraga managed to avert disaster by evolving his unique, evocative idiosyncratic vision and by manipulating and imbuing it with the powerful juxtaposition of technique and materials that make his paintings so disquieting. If one gleans the impression that his painting is intuitively effortless it is the result of his determined, scrupulous intellectual grasp of painting. Fraga might think of himself as a folk painter engaging the collective subconscious, but he is too accomplished, sophisticated and successful to genuinely make that claim; most of the work in this retrospective is drawn from forty-two private collections and museums. However, because of his maverick determination to make narrative images on the cusp of the secular/sacred rift, his work, once it has cast its spell, appeals more to the soul than to the whims of a superficial glance. But more than his technical tenacity, it is his love of painting and conviction about images that make Ed Fraga a truly visionary artist.

Dick Goody   Director, Meadow Brook Art Gallery

Discarded objects that speak of past lives are strewn across the cityscape. A used door or window frame becomes a house for a portrait or land-scape. A saintly, haunting face peers through a portal, enveloped by a light that suggests an unearthtly place and time.

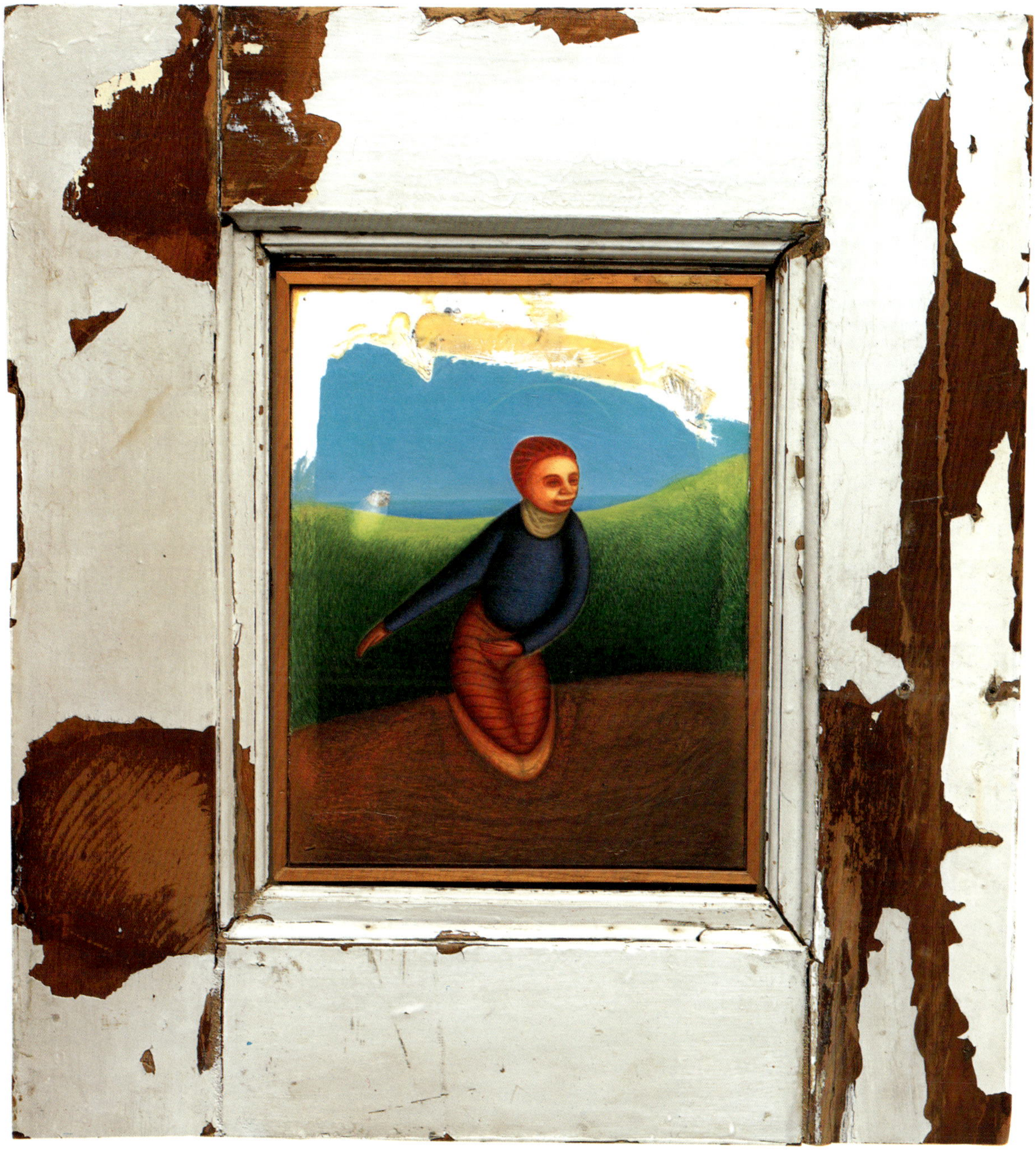

Aisreal [1] 1987
oil, tape on paper mounted on wood, found frame 23½ x 21 x 2¼ inches
Collection of Wendy MacGaw and Ted Lee Hadfield, Farmington Hills, MI

INJURY

MY interest in illusion grew out of a fascination with magic. As a child I remember reading books on the subject. I took this knowledge and performed various death defying acts to a small audience, which usually turned out to be my brother and sisters and an occasional neighborhood friend.

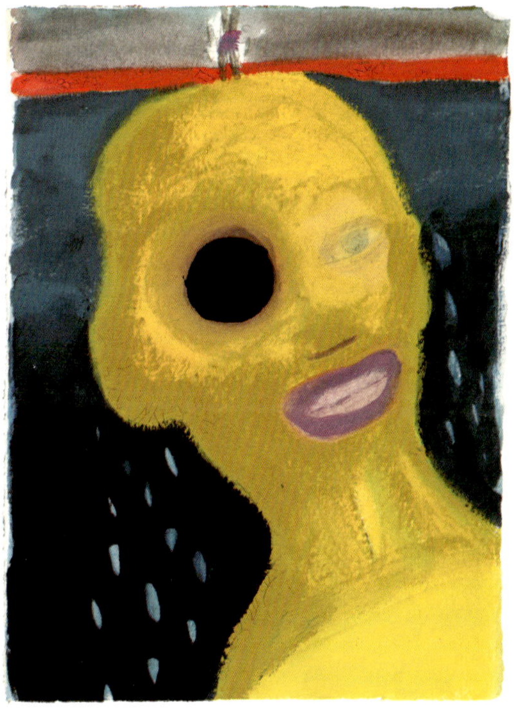

I often think art resembles magic; the trick to both is to create an illusion by drawing the viewer into your world and suspend their disbelief, if only for a while. The desire is that the visual experience will resonate for some time after.

As early as two years old, I experienced my first trauma having burned my leg in a backyard trash burning accident. I became aware quite early that accidental fate would be a way of life for me. I had a prophetic, foreboding sense of my own vulnerability. It was not until age twelve that this prophecy came to life. While cutting rope (to attach a pulley on the back of my brother's wagon) the knife slipped and cut my right eye. It was this crucial accident that would ironically direct my destiny.

With vision permanently impaired, the impetus to create became even greater. I recall, with vivid detail, how I would create worlds of fantasy by taking simple shoeboxes and transform them into theatrical stage sets. I would gather toys and various disparate materials to invent dramas that told a story. Later, I wrote plays and suspense thrillers based on the suggestive narratives.

One Eyed Swimmer 1981 water color on paper 7 x 5 inches

RETABLO

IN Mexico, once a year, death is celebrated in the midst of life. Each autumn, the living invite their dead to join them in a festival of communion - to return home again and, for a few hours, to sit by the hearth and warm their cold bones before returning to the land of the dead.[1]

During 1994 I exhibited a multi-media work at the Cranbrook Art Museum entitled *The Isenheim Interior*. Inspired by the *Isenheim Altar* by 15th c. German painter Grünewald, the installation I created not only paid homage to this great work but also re-contextualized the poignancy and relevancy of the past with the present as it related to issues of disease and death. The work memorialized past lives and explored the ephemeral nature of life and the intrinsic human desire for beauty. It employed paintings, sculpture, and appropriation. *The Isenheim Interior* was a sacred space in which a ritual had just concluded and all that remained were the artifacts used during the service. It was the moment after the sacred event, and the visitor had to reconstruct the drama using the sets and props that remained.

This notion of art/artifact in the guise of talisman is deeply rooted in many primitive and civilized cultures. The Latin tradition of retablo (altarpiece, or as commonly referred to as ex-votos) painting is one such example of the role visual imagery plays as mediator to divine forces. Usually painted on tin, these small icons are created by amateur artists to petition saints for guidance against illness. The beauty of these folk paintings is in their expressed innocence and unpretentious bravado. They are revelations of the heart. Text often accompanies these paintings, which clearly expresses specific pleas by the petitioner. When the prayer is answered, the retablo is placed at the altar of a church as an offering of thanksgiving. A candle is also lit.

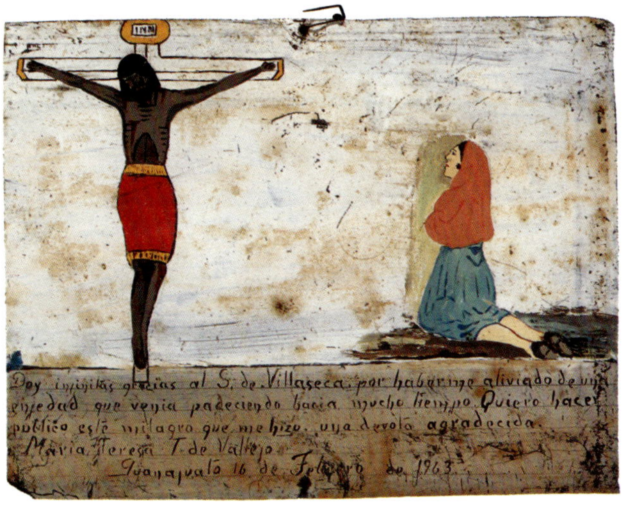

My drawings and paintings draw upon affinities with this art form, especially much of the early work, which addresses issues such as disease and death, fear and anxiety. Employing a single, solipsistic figure to occupy the barren landscape in many of the paintings from this period reinforced the sense of vulnerability and isolation.

T. de Vallejo, *Untitled Retablo* 1963 oil on tin Collection of Tim Thayer

PANTHEISM

A paradoxical juxtaposition exists between darkness and light in the paintings *Winter Resurrection 1* (page 31) and *La Santa E Gloriosa Carne* (page 44). The suggestive narratives allude to the eternal and the divine, calling upon the viewer to project a spirit of hope against a background of despair. Christian themes are evident in the titles of many paintings, drawing upon the iconography of the Medieval and Renaissance periods. It is a continual challenge to readdress historical religious subject matter in ways that bring new relevancy and poignancy to the subject. A reverence for all that is sacred is portended in many works whether it is expressed by the inner light that resonates from a lush, fertile landscape or in the yearning to be born anew by an androgynous-looking figure. This idea of the spiritual is not limited to the western belief system and quite often embraces eastern philosophies of Hinduism. I frequently employ serpentine-like organisms in my paintings. The snake embodies many different meanings as a symbol in art. In the Judaic-Christian tradition, the snake represents temptation or evil; whereas in Hinduism, the snake, which sheds its skin many times in its life, is viewed as a symbol of renewal and rebirth.

ALCHEMY

The process of making art has always seemed analogous to alchemy in that the success of a work of art relies heavily on the ability to manipulate materials with the result being the transformation of the mundane into the miraculous.

Living and working in Detroit during the 80's and 90's influenced the art I produced. The city was and still is a playground of discarded, postindustrial refuse. The past surrounds the city. Strewn across the barren cityscape lie discarded mutations of urban blight. Newly formed hybrids of crumbling buildings meld with automobile parts. Finding a paint-peeled wall or door in a back alley or abandoned field, weathered by time, held the same excitement as discovering a fossilized rock for me as a child. With their own unique patinas, I could see the potential these discarded relics of the past had for staging a narrative of the bizarre, with figures as the characters and landscapes as the backdrops to various allegorical dramas.

In my first solo exhibition at the Feigenson Gallery in 1982, I incorporated found objects: door and mirror frames, broken panes of glass, animal teeth, into hermetically sealed reliquaries. These icons, as they were called, encased oil pastel drawings of homeless people I observed on the streets. Relying on memory, I would isolate moments in time that caught my curiosity, like when I saw a crazy lady wearing a plastic bag over her head screaming obscenities as she paced back and forth. Or the time, on a late summer night in August, I recall meeting some friends at a restaurant in Hamtramck; a friendly, but tired waitress served us a round of hot dogs at *Geenie's Weenies* (page 18).

[1] Rosalind Rosoff Beimler, *Los Dias de Muertos*

Ed Fraga, 2001

PORTRAITS

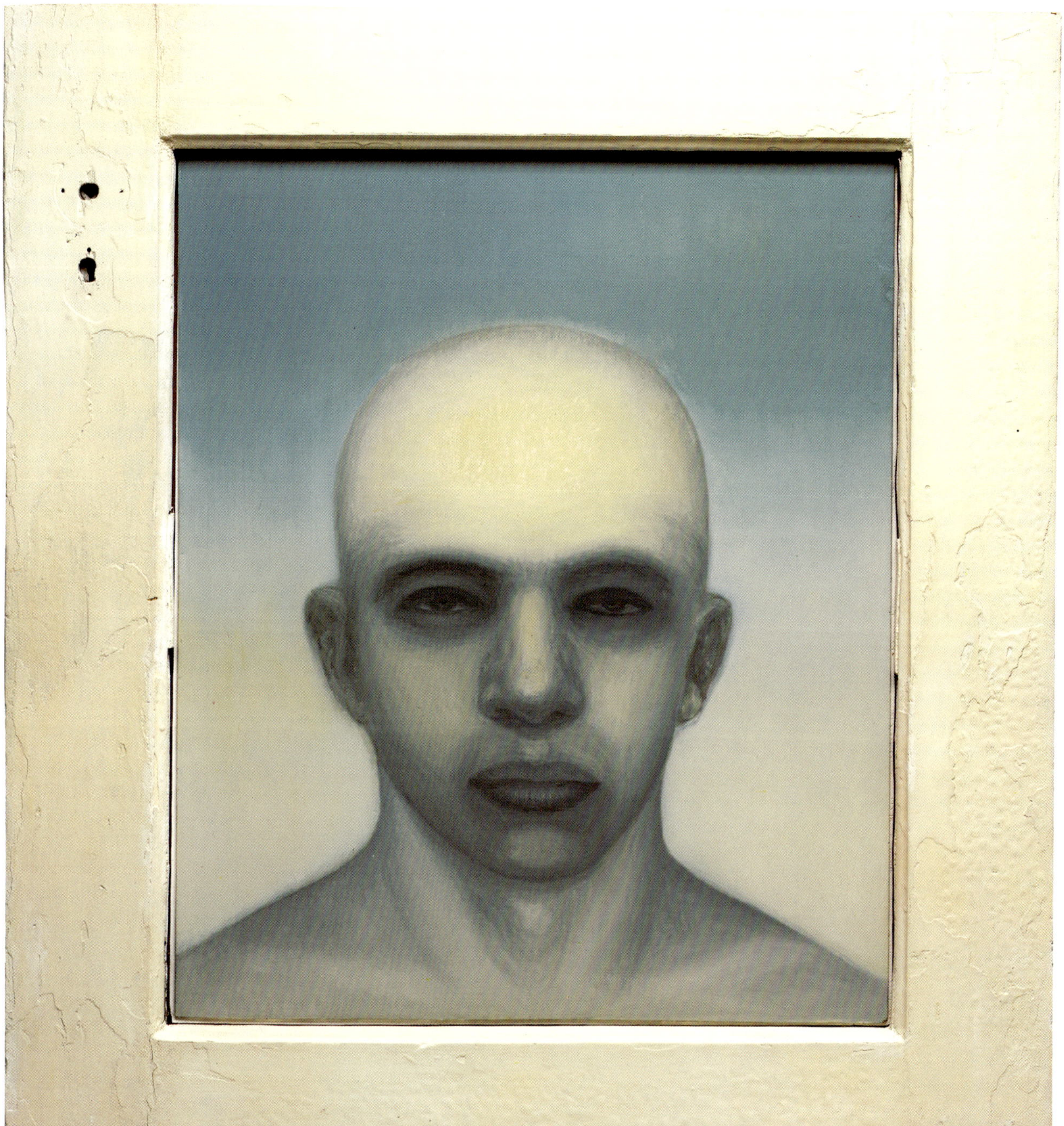

Remembrance 1992
oil on wood 32 x 30 x 2 inches
Collection of Leo Maxbauer, West Bloomfield, MI

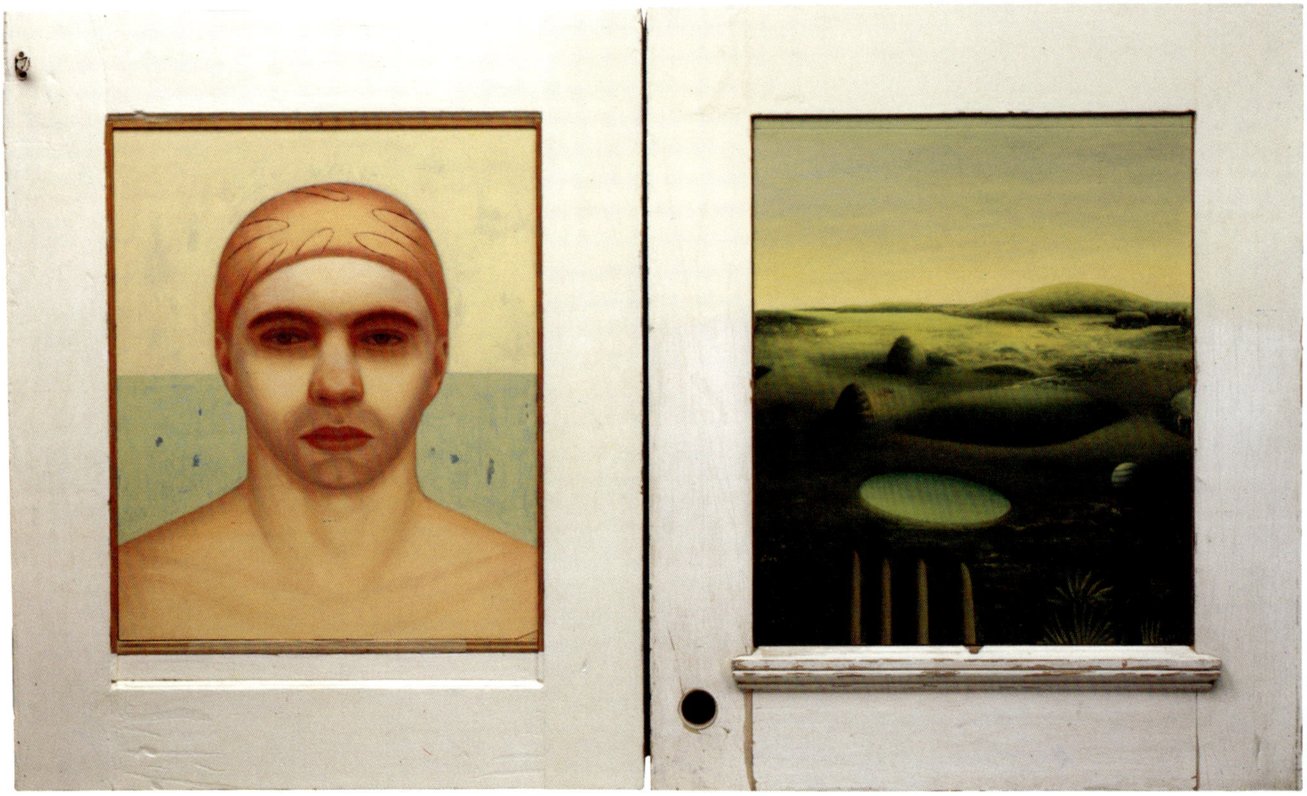

Stone'em/Bury'em 1991
oil on wood 35 x 54 x 3 inches
Collection of Gayle and Andrew Camden, Detroit, MI

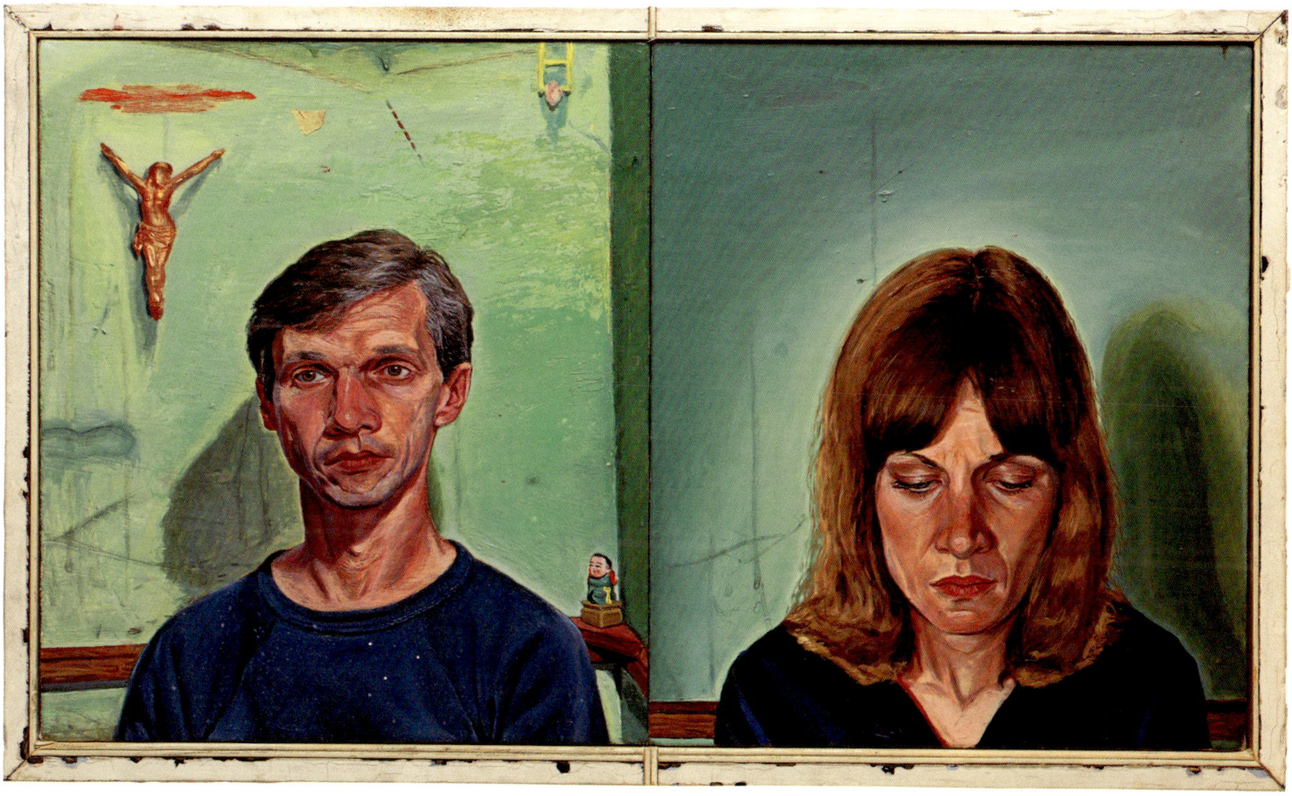

George and Ann 1982
oil on canvas 15 x 26 inches
Private Collection

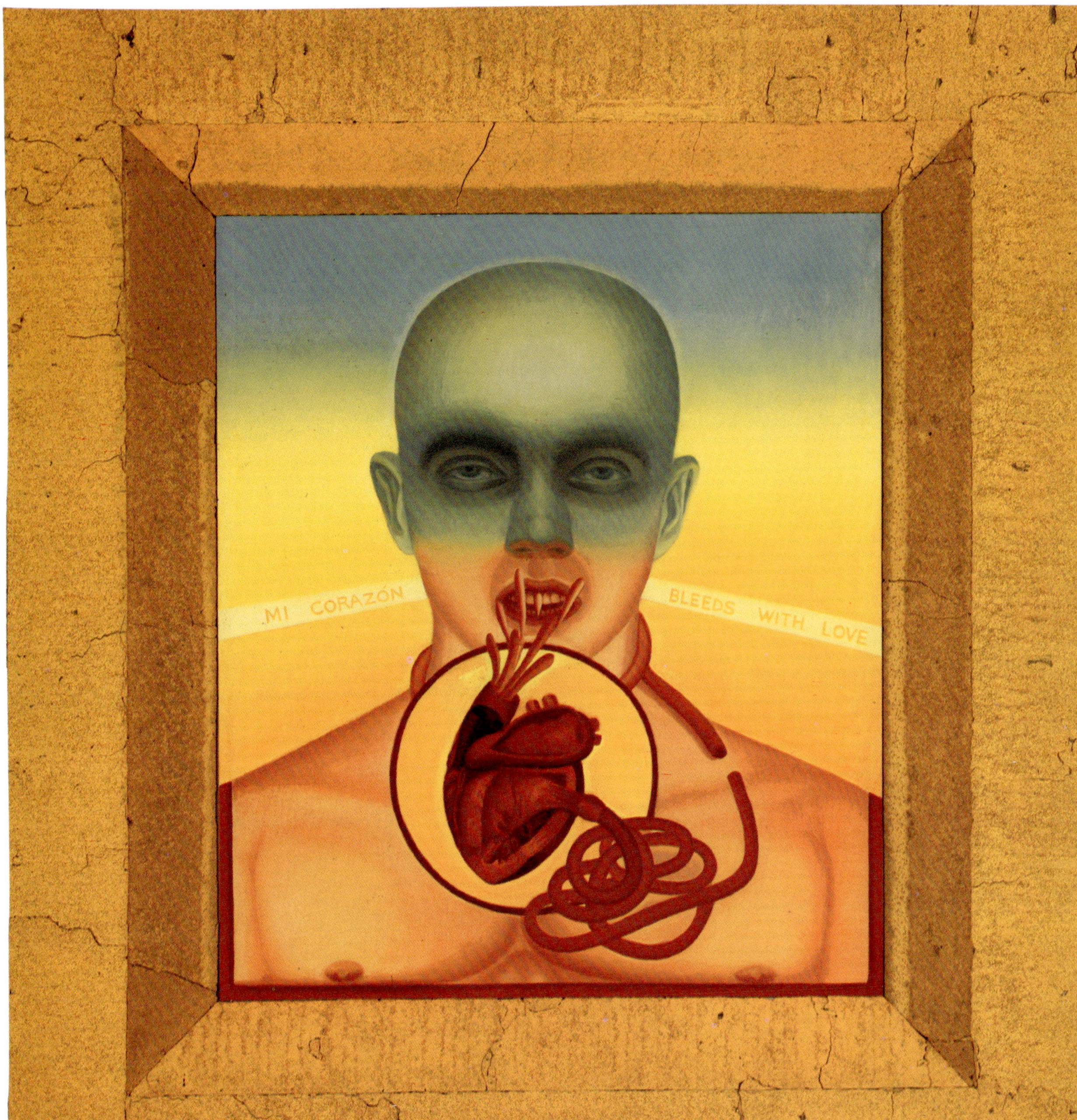

Mi Corazón 1993
oil on wood, highway median 42 x 38 x 4 inches
Collection of the Artist

BLOOD
COURSING THROUGH
MY VEINS CHANGING
FROM BLUE TO RED
AS IT KISSES
THE AIR

ICONS

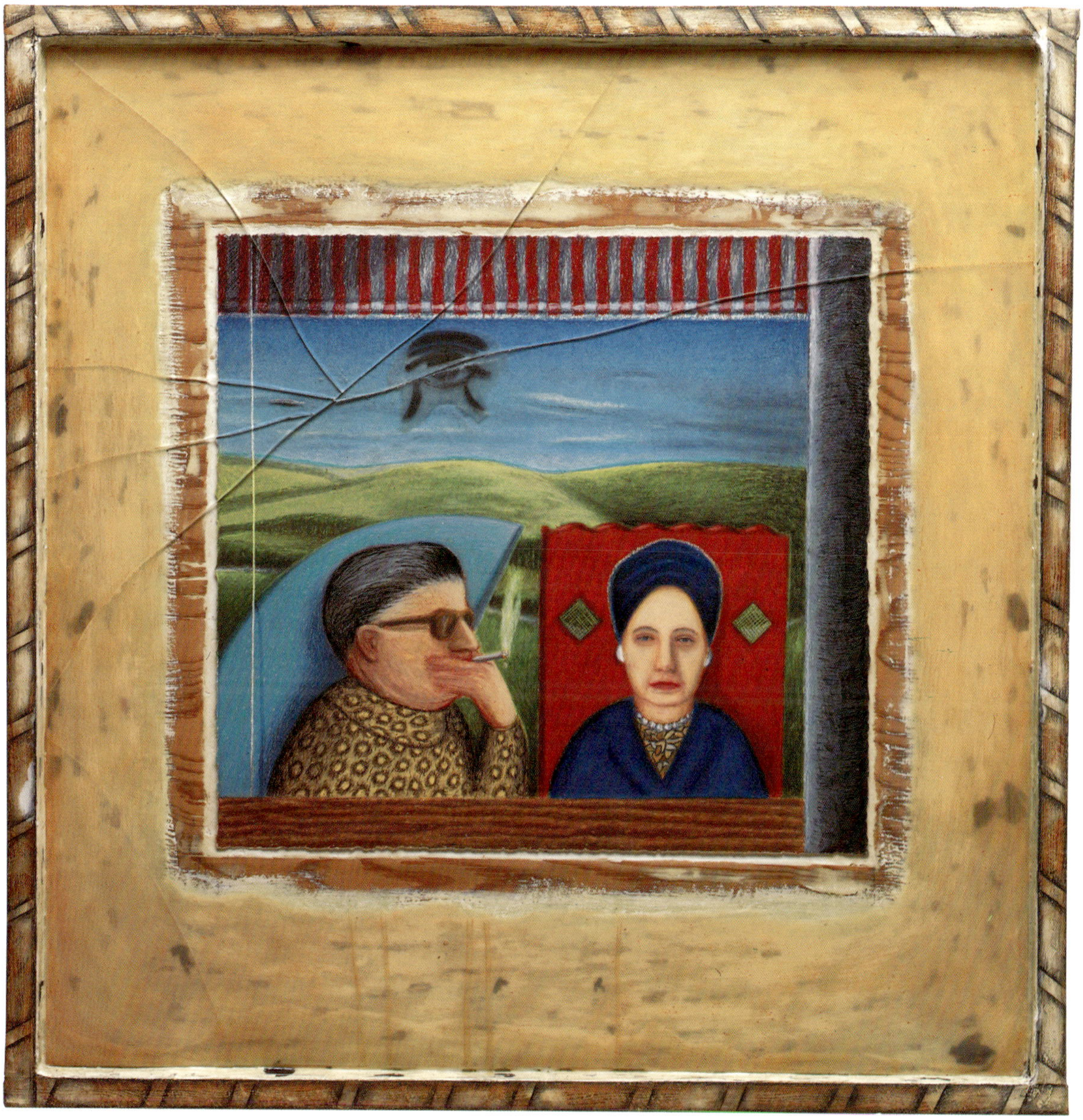

Stagefright 1983
oil pastel, paper, wood, glue, glass 27 x 26 x 1½ inches
Collection of Judy Primak, Detroit, MI

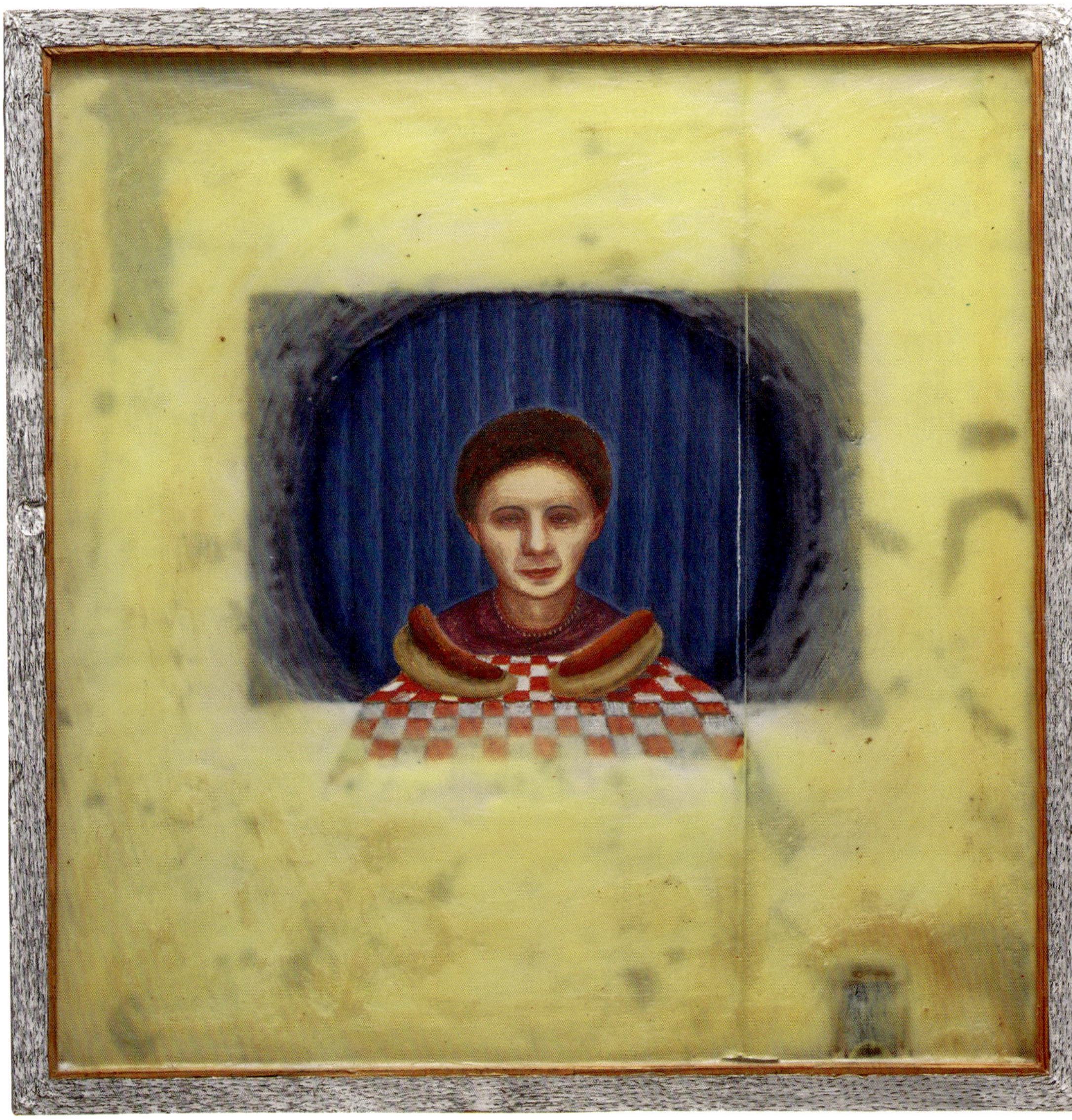

Geenie's Weenies 1983
oil pastel, paper, wood, wax, glass 20 x 20 x 1½ inches
Collection of Eliot and Elizabeth Bank, Columbus, OH

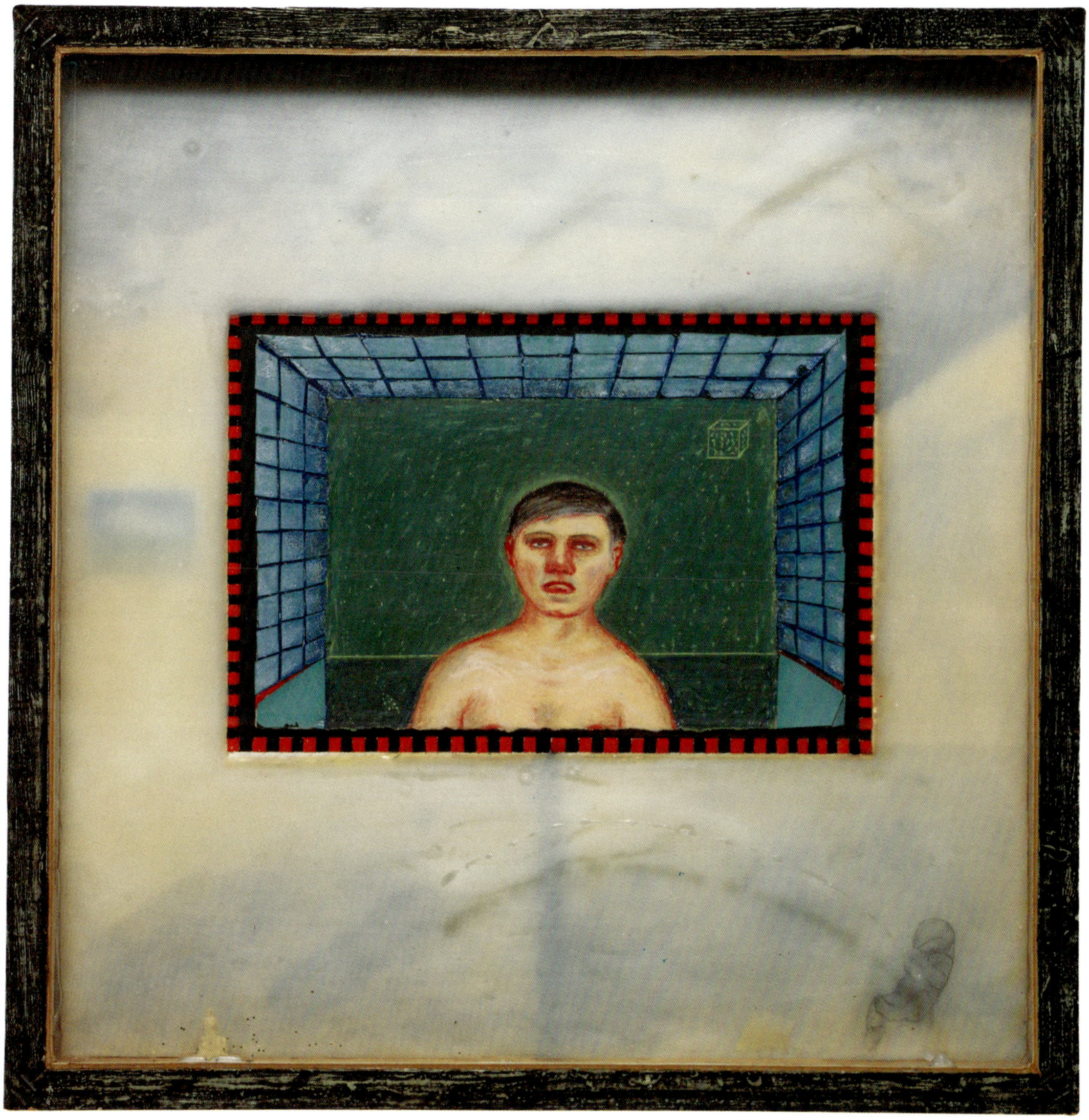

Diagnosis Glass 1983
oil pastel, paper, wood, glue, glass 20 x 20 x 1½ inches
Collection of David Zucca, Ann Arbor, MI

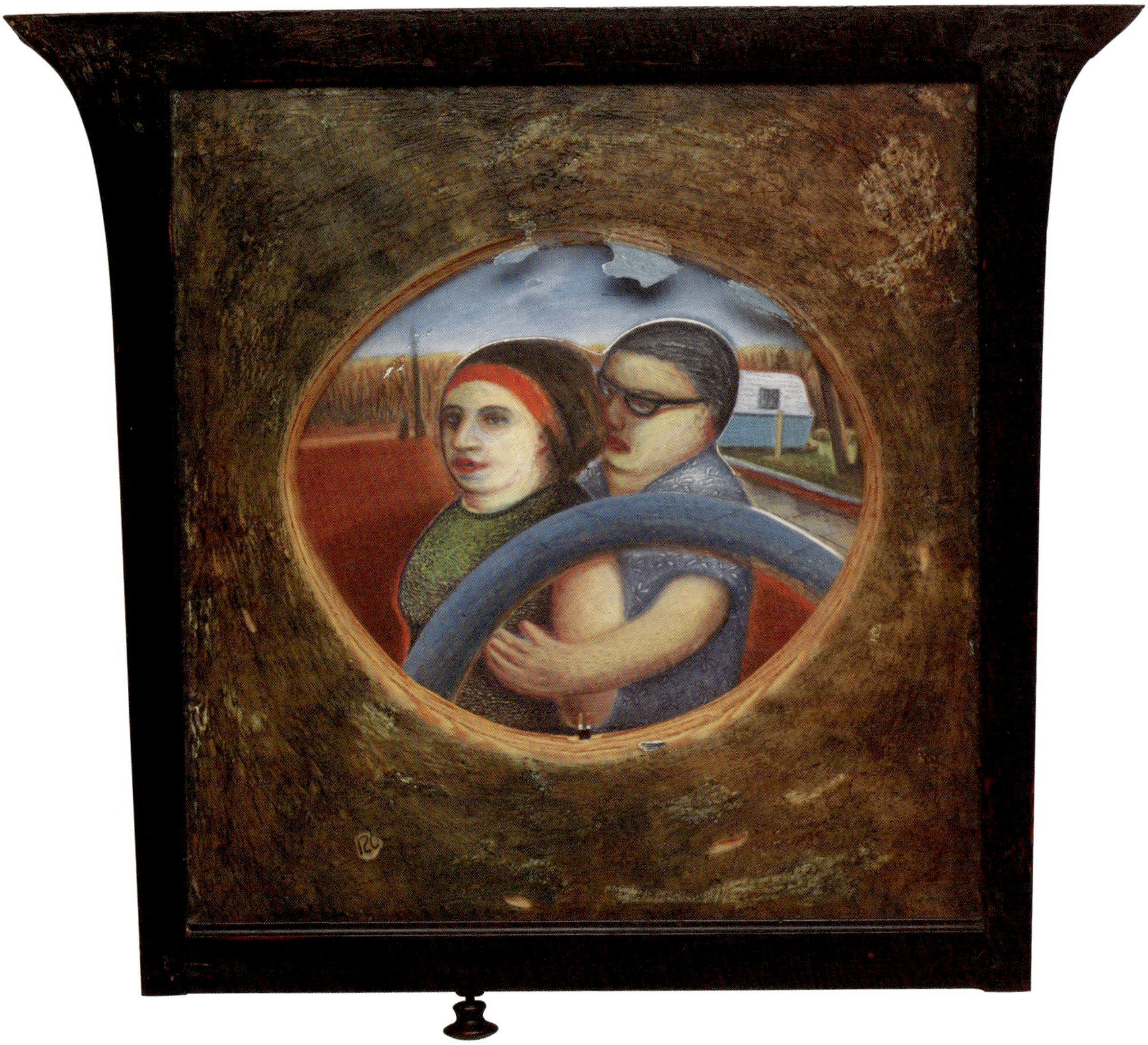

One Two Zero 1983
oil pastel, paper, wood, wax, glass 22 x 24 x 1½ inches
Collection of Roy Castleberry, Royal Oak, MI

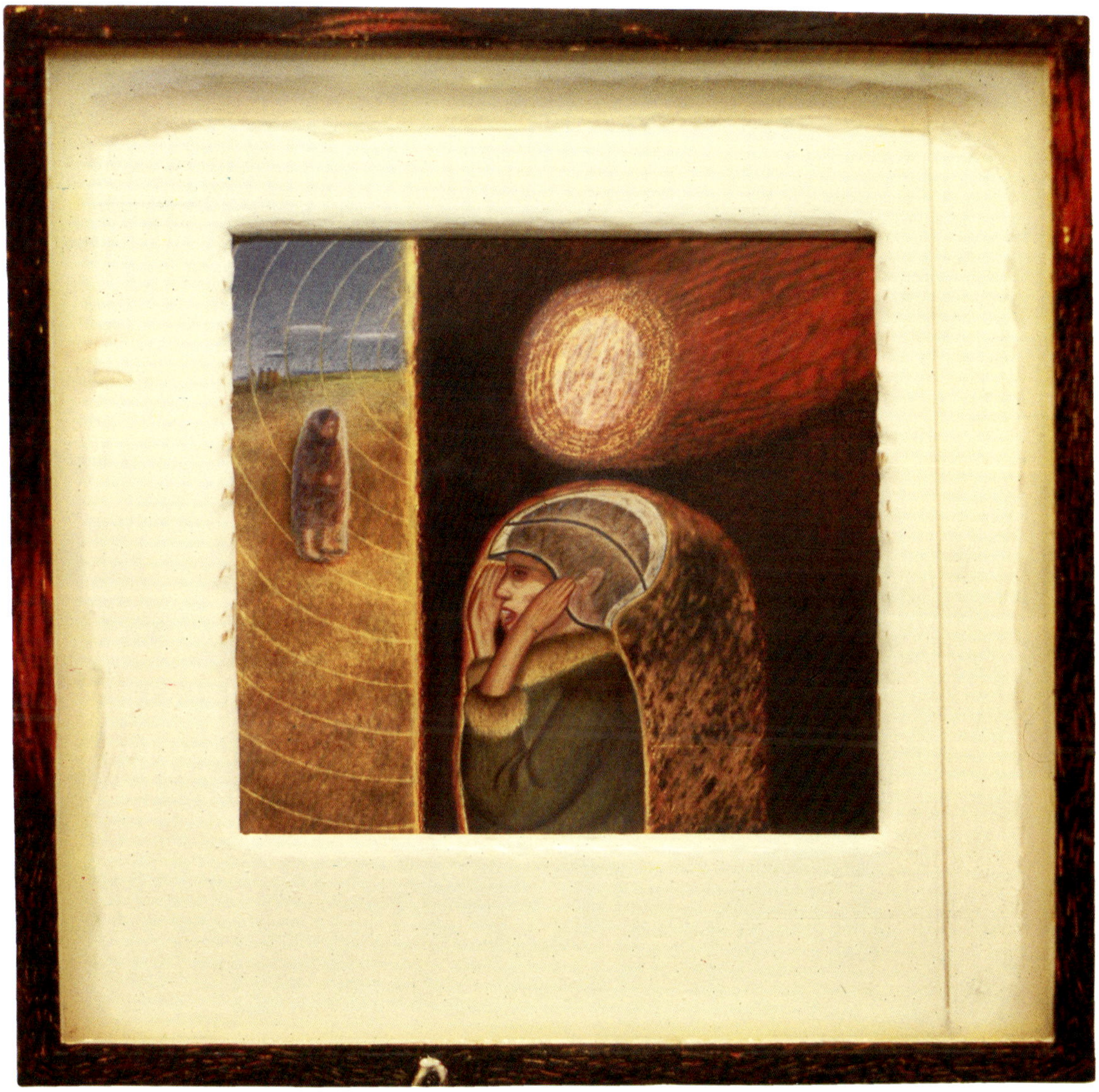

Only the Mandorla will Save Her 1984
oil pastel, paper, wood, string, deer tooth, glass 26 x 26 x 3 inches
Collection of Meg Cox, Princeton, NJ

RELIQUARIES

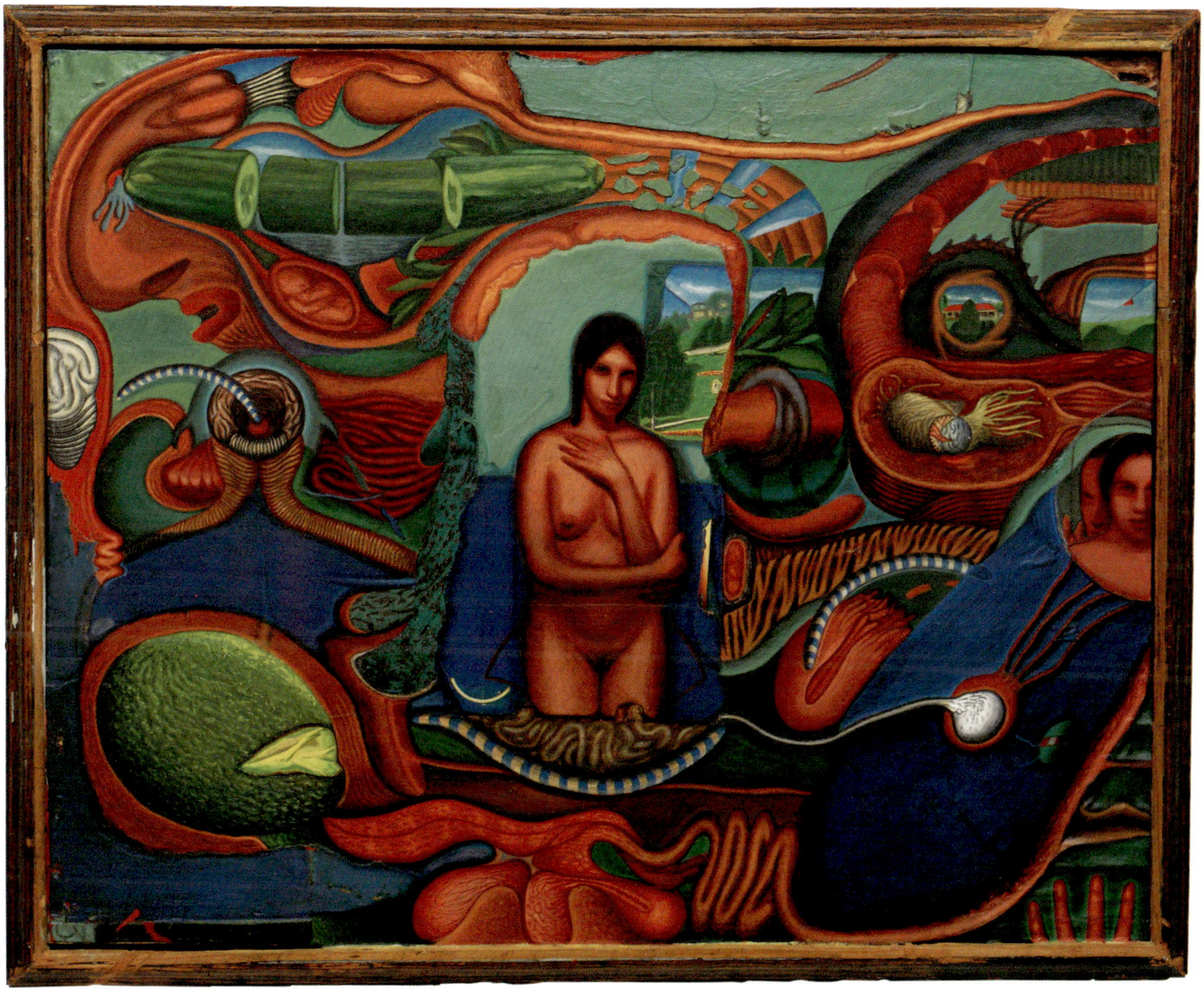

Untitled 1984
oil, photocollage, pencil, wood 17 x 20 inches
Collection of Tom Humes, Detroit, MI

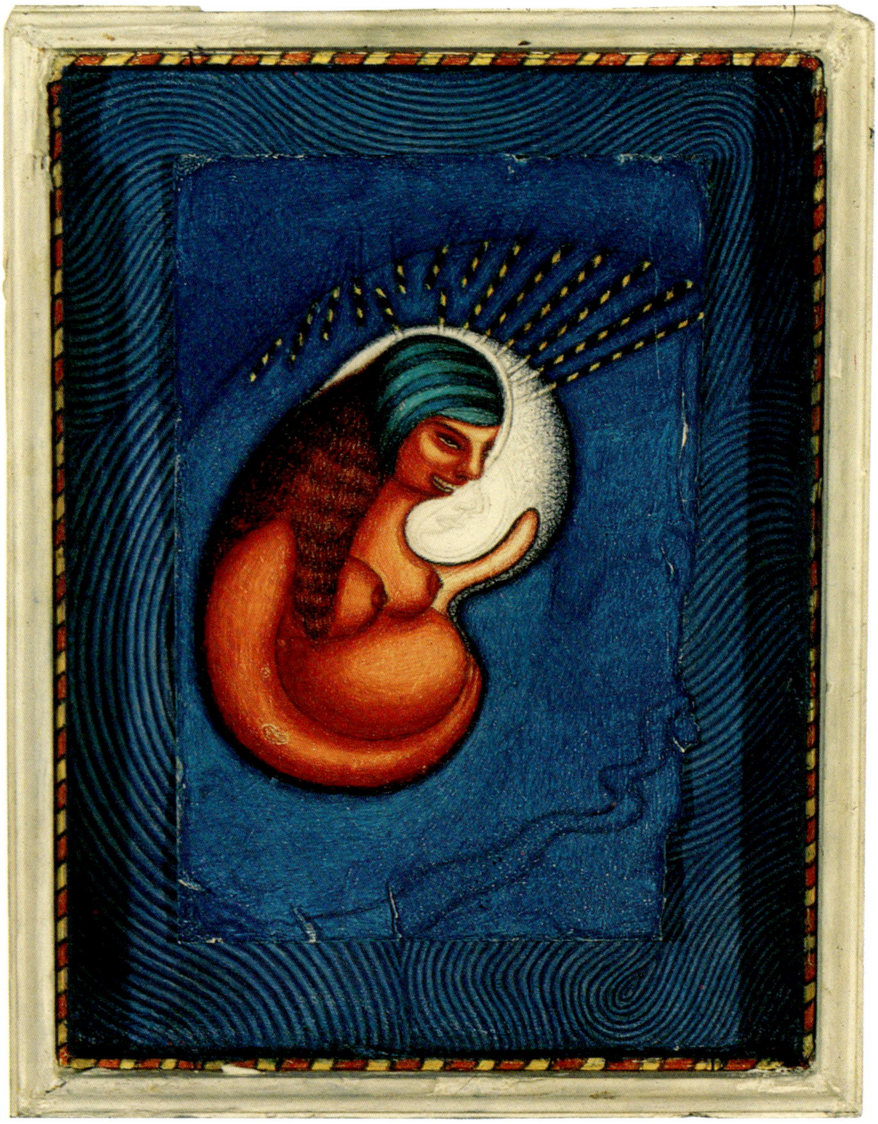

229 Gratiot (detail above) 1986
photograph, pencil, oil, crayon, glass, wood on plasterboard
35½ x 34¼ x 2¼ inches
Collection of Andronike A. Tsagaris and John D. Hilberry, NewYork, NY

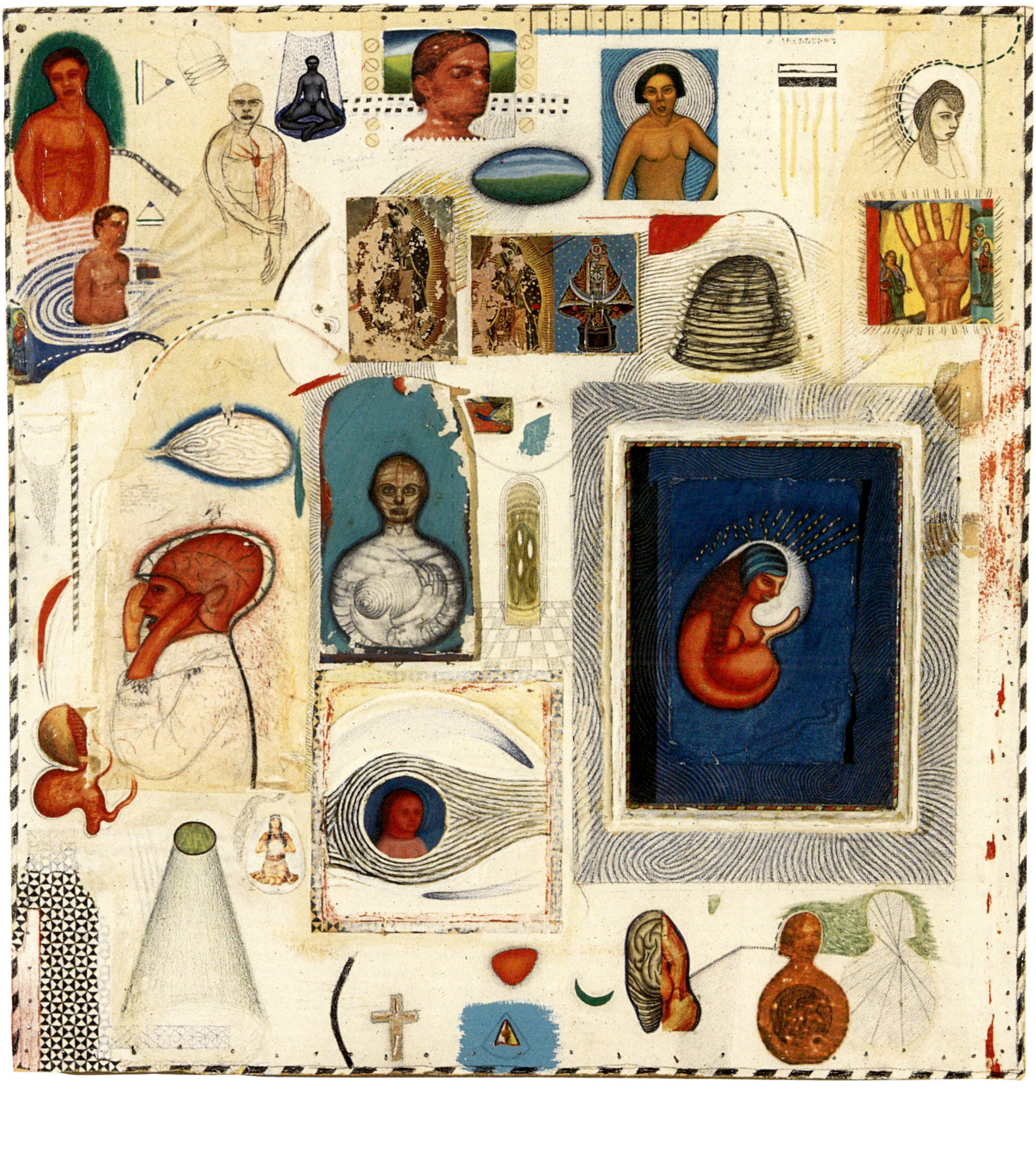

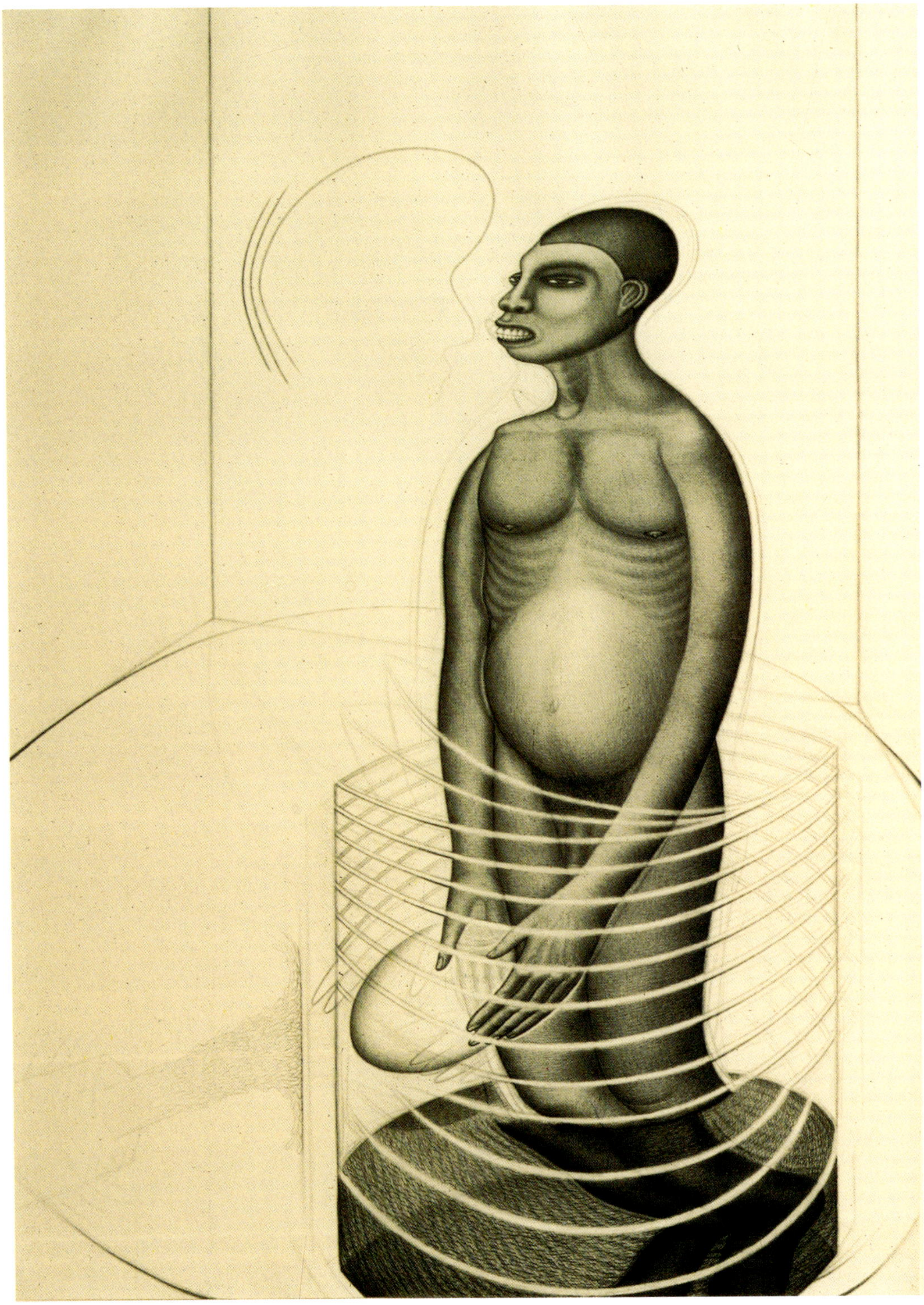

Temporary Ruler 1986
pencil on paper 56 x 41 inches
Privated Collection

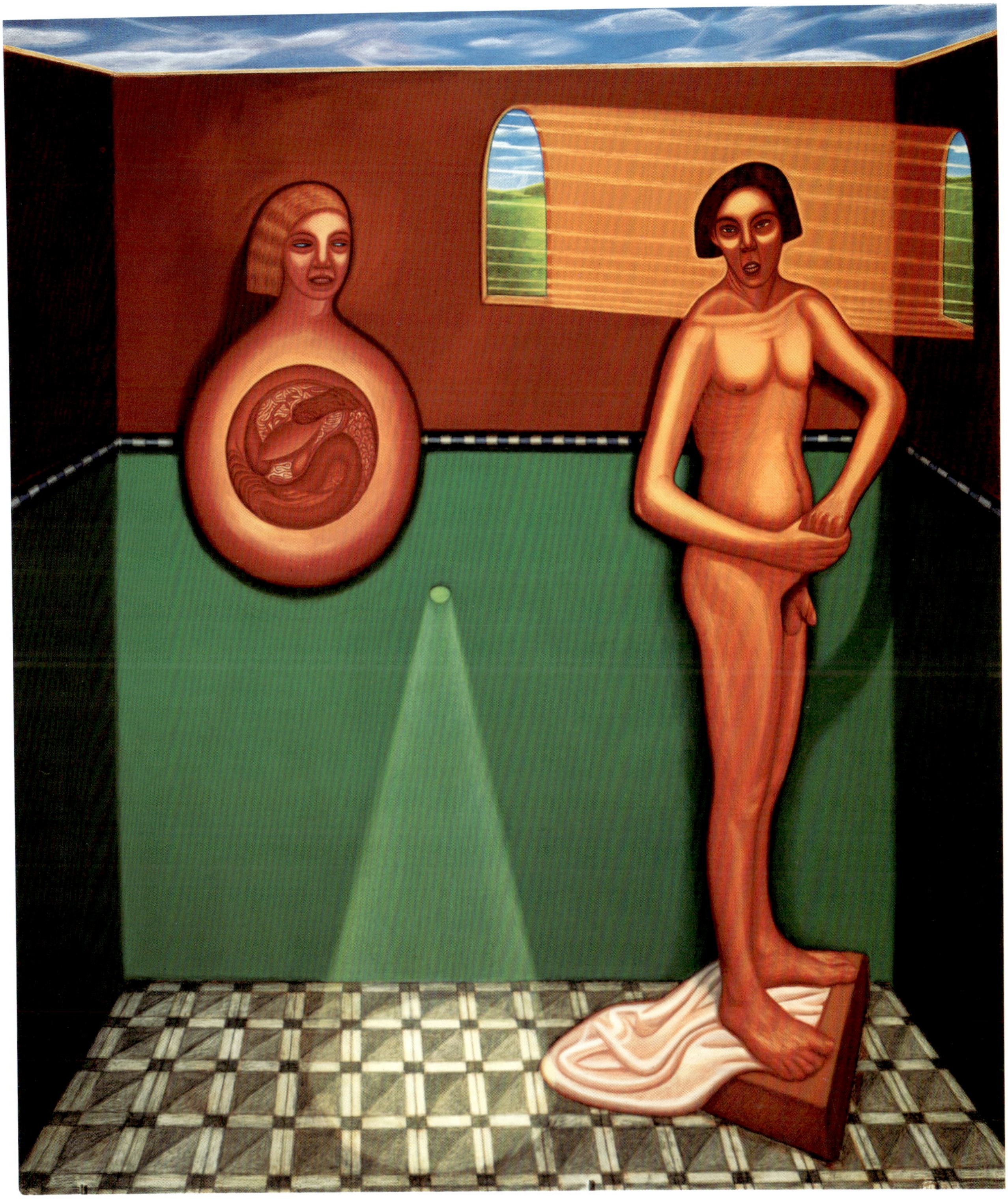

False Light 1985
oil and color pencil on wood 67 x 63 inches
Collection of the Artist

ALTARS TO THE SEASONS

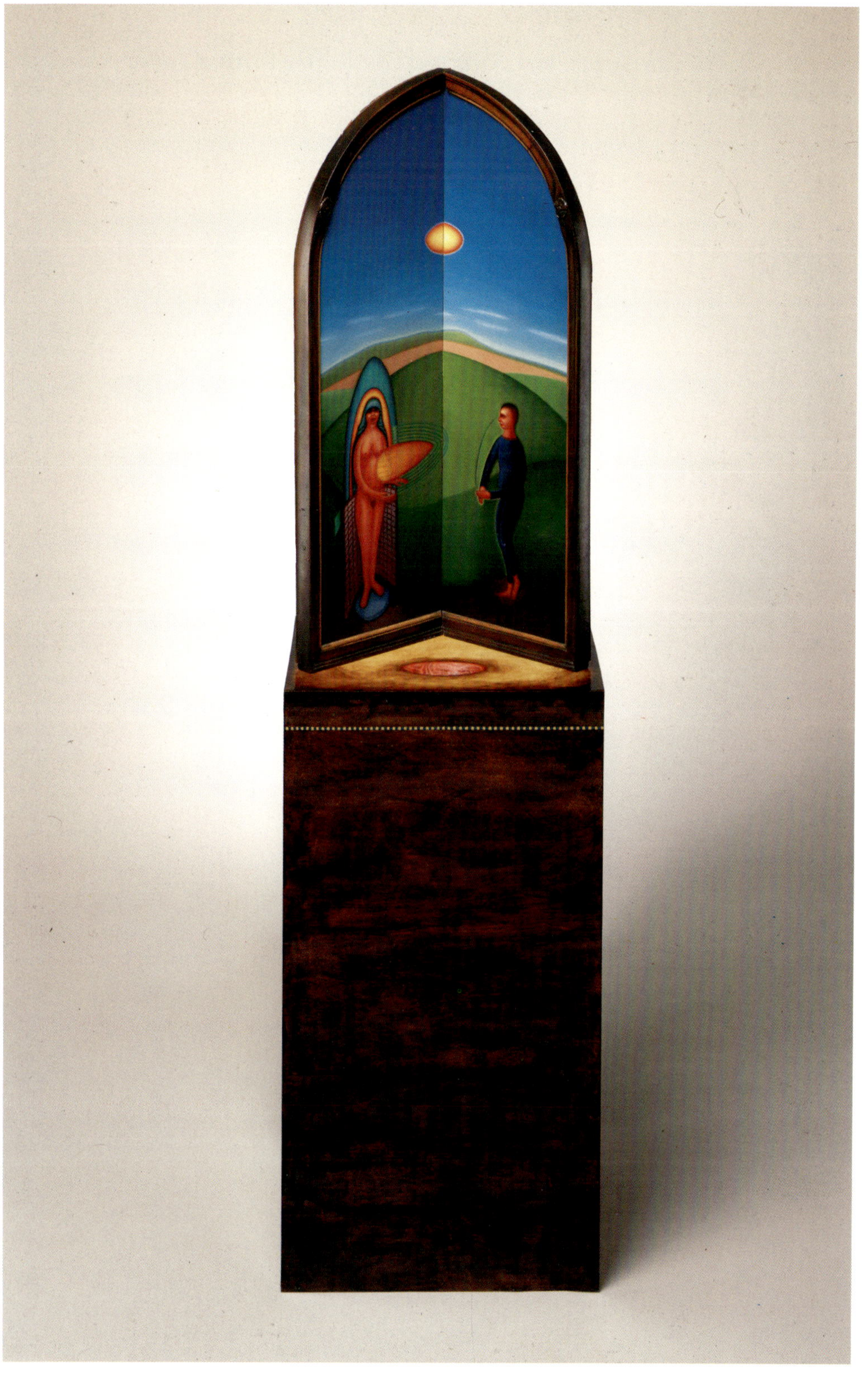

Summer 1986
oil on wood 67 x 18 x 14 inches
Collection of Tim Thayer and Grace Serra, Detroit, MI

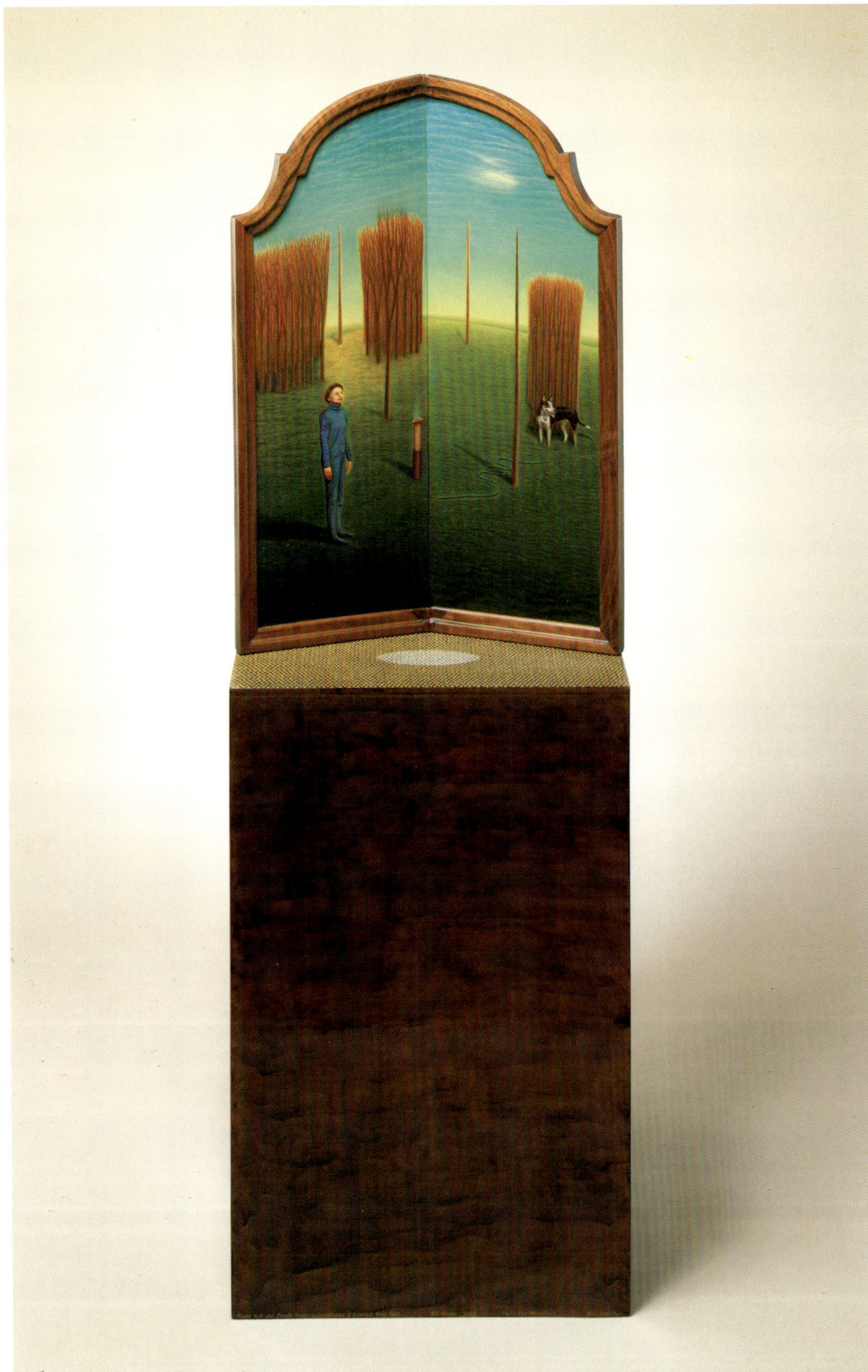

Fall - The Marriage 1987
oil on wood 64" x 18" x 13"
Collection of Marilyn Zimmerman, Ferndale, MI

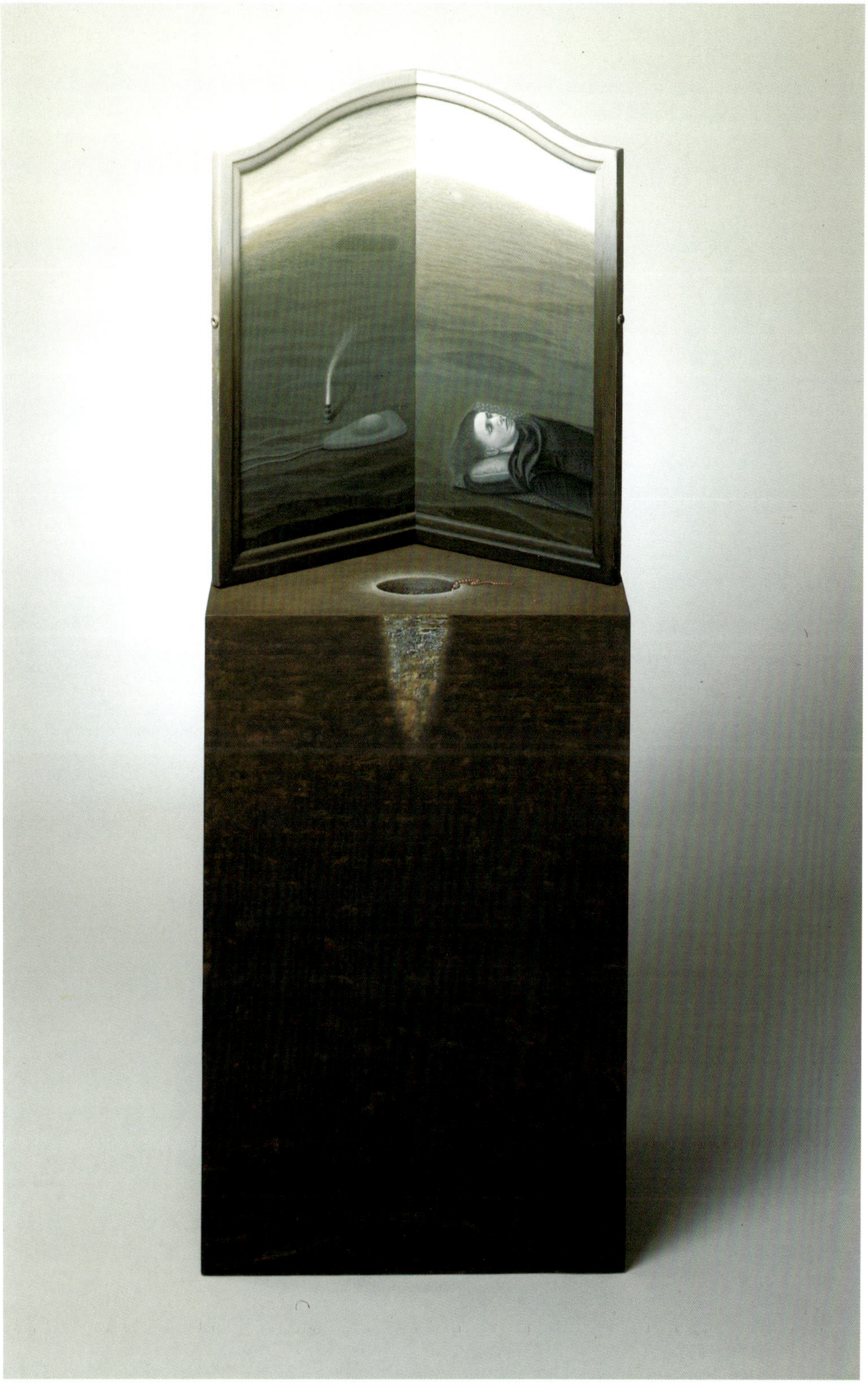

Winter - Resurrection 1988
oil on wood 61 x 22 x 13 inches
Collection of the Artist

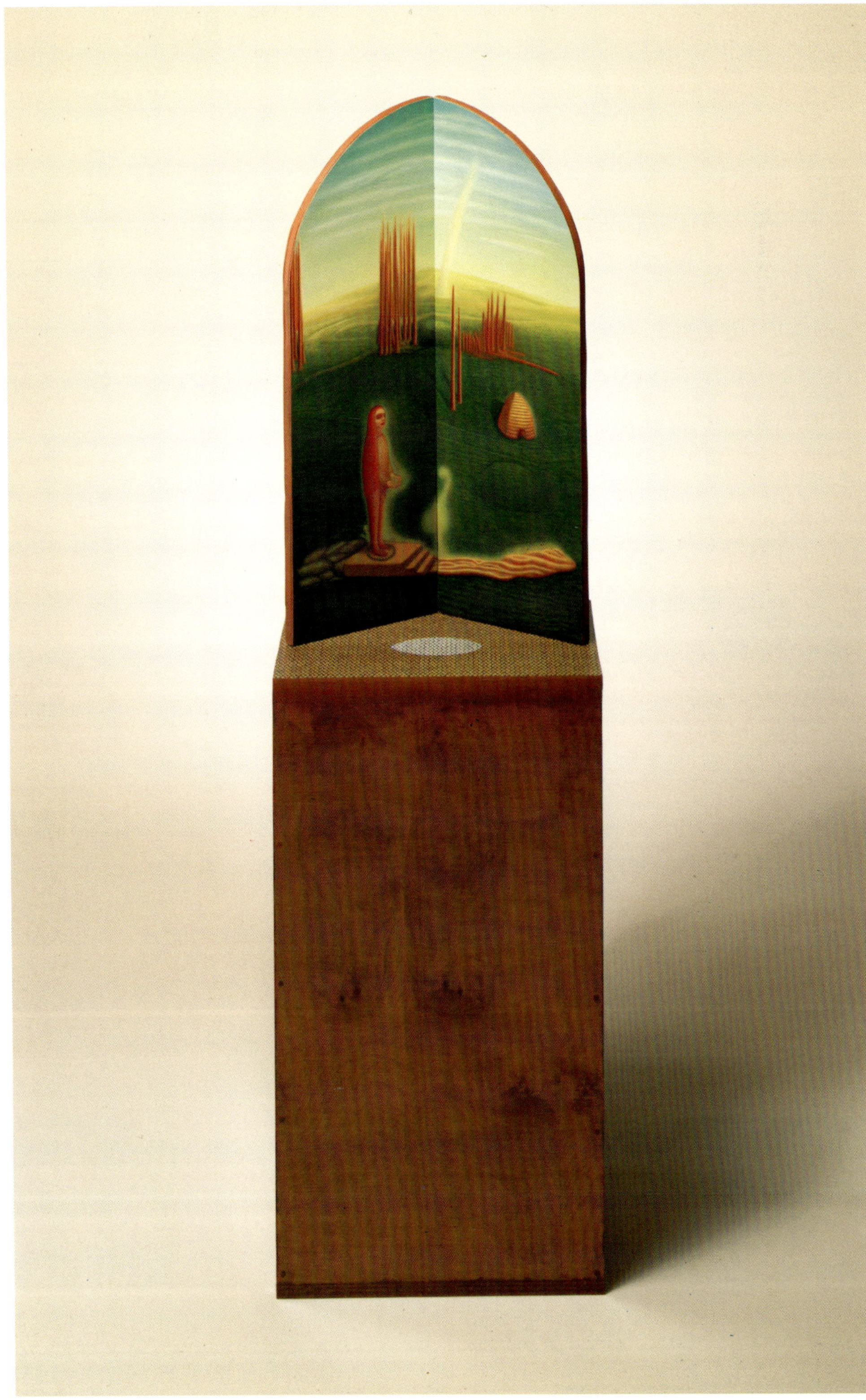

Spring - Transfiguration 1988
oil on wood 64 x 18 x 13 inches
Collection of Vivian Day and John Stroh III, Grosse Pointe, MI

PAINTINGS 1989-1990

Ed Fraga's paintings make the strange appear familiar and the familiar strange. They seem to be pictures of places one has seen before although it is difficult to quite remember where or when. Upon closer observation, these same places become ever more foreign, until finally they are unlike anything that could possibly be experienced in the real world. The world Fraga explores is that of the unconscious, specifically the world of dreams with its power to influence and shape events beyond the control of the human mind.

Fraga's paintings, not unlike the "Magic Realism" style of painting of the 1930's, are precise, realistic presentations of an ordinary scene with no strange or monstrous distortion; the magic arises from the intensity of the struggle between emotion and repression. In the four large paintings from 1990 that constitute his first important series – *Eniskuo, Floating Man, Sinking Man, and Omnipresent Hand* – the human in each sense is absorbed into the environment, melding with the stylized land masses and vegetation that describe the landscape. In *Floating Man*, the most beautiful and resolved of the series, a man floats on his back in a pool of still water, his lower torso hidden by what appears to be a portion of a barrel. Across the shimmering landscape up to the elevated horizon line, planks of wood, perhaps additional barrel staves, follow single file. A weak sun shines in the direct center of the grey area at the arched top of the painting. The key to unlock Fraga's images can be found in *Eniskuo*, which takes its name from a Greek word that means "to make inwardly strong." Fraga is greatly attracted by the idea of attempting to express inner strength through his withdrawn, trancelike figures. The figures' eyes - the "windows of the soul" – in each of the four paintings are either closed or sightlessly glazed, repressing personality and emotion. The figures must depend only on the eerie strength of their own humanity to distinguish them from the landscape.

The human figure in a kind of psychic suspension has been a common theme in Fraga's work. His paintings from the mid-1980s placed a heavily outlined figure, often seated cross-legged in a mystic or prayerful pose. The visually shocking palette of secondary colors - oranges, yellow-greens, and intense violet-blues – belies the scene's repose. In later paintings the sense of emotional calm is enhanced by a lighter, more complex, even glowing color scheme, in which warm, soft golds and delicate clear blues and greens predominate. The painting thus takes on a sense of quiet withdrawal, even a hushed breathlessness as in the pregnant moment between a flash of lightning and the resulting thunderclap. Fraga has described this as "the moment before the bomb goes off, the moment before something happens." That "something" is likely to be a metaphysical or psychological event: a resurrection, a release of the soul through death, or, less dramatically, a new understanding of the self. The figures' poses - sinking, floating, half-buried – relate them directly to other landscape forms and indicate the potential for harmony between humans and nature; that is, if the conscious mind can be released to allow the unconscious to take over. The silent, private world inhabited by Fraga's subjects has neither a place for communion with the living world nor communication of thought. One draws upon one's own inner strength, developed through trust of the natural world.

Earlier construction paintings also demonstrate Fraga's interest in exploring the mind as an inner, private world. In these works, an opaque material such as wood or strips of road tar is place over a painting of a figure in a landscape. A small oval aperture is then cut into the covering, allowing just a glimpse of the painting underneath. Like Alice in *Through the Looking-Glass*, we can then see into a magical world that is physically inaccessible to us. The fragment of landscape revealed through the oval is perfectly crafted, meticulously painted, and rigorously ordered, receding into the far distance from deep middle ground. Silhouetted against it is a figure in the immediate foreground. This model, and indeed even the delicate, painstaking rendering of the landscape itself, is reminiscent of Italian Quattrocento portraiture, such as that of Botticelli or Ghirlandaio. The connection with earlier portrait conventions becomes all the more compelling when one realizes that the face used in most of Fraga's paintings is his own. Although it has been noted by some observers that self-portraiture is more prominent in the new series than earlier paintings, I would suggest that the faces in Fraga's work are always his own, in feature if not in demeanor. The artist himself then stands in for the rest of us as a traveler in both mind and body.

Ed Fraga's mystical landscapes have a powerful pull. Inhabited or not, their seductive tension draws us in with feelings of fear and wonder. The natural world as enemy and friend has been a popular theme among American painters, and Fraga explores this conundrum to develop his own sense of power.

MaryAnn Wilkinson

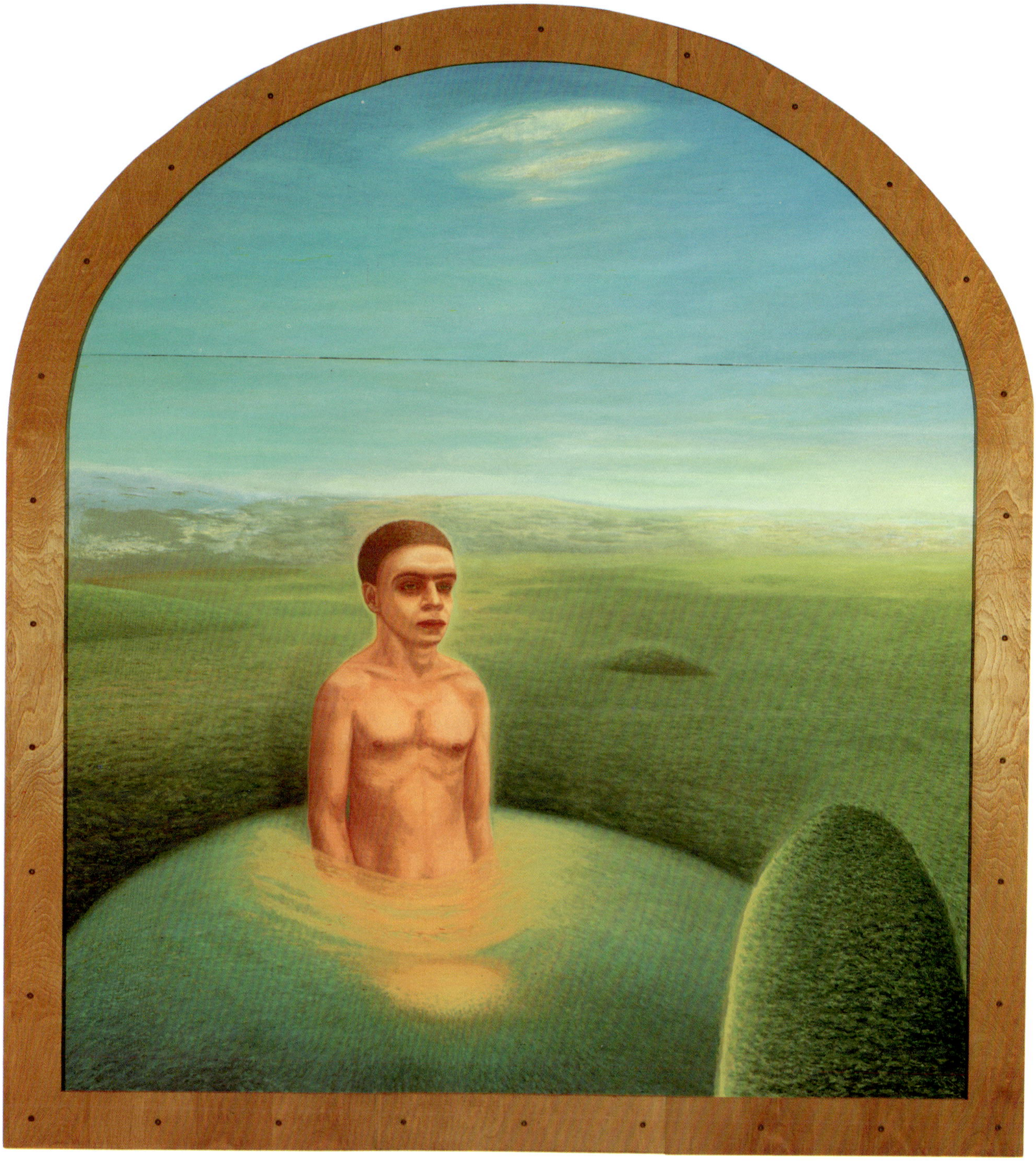

Sinking Man 1989
oil on wood 75 x 67 inches
Collection of the Artist

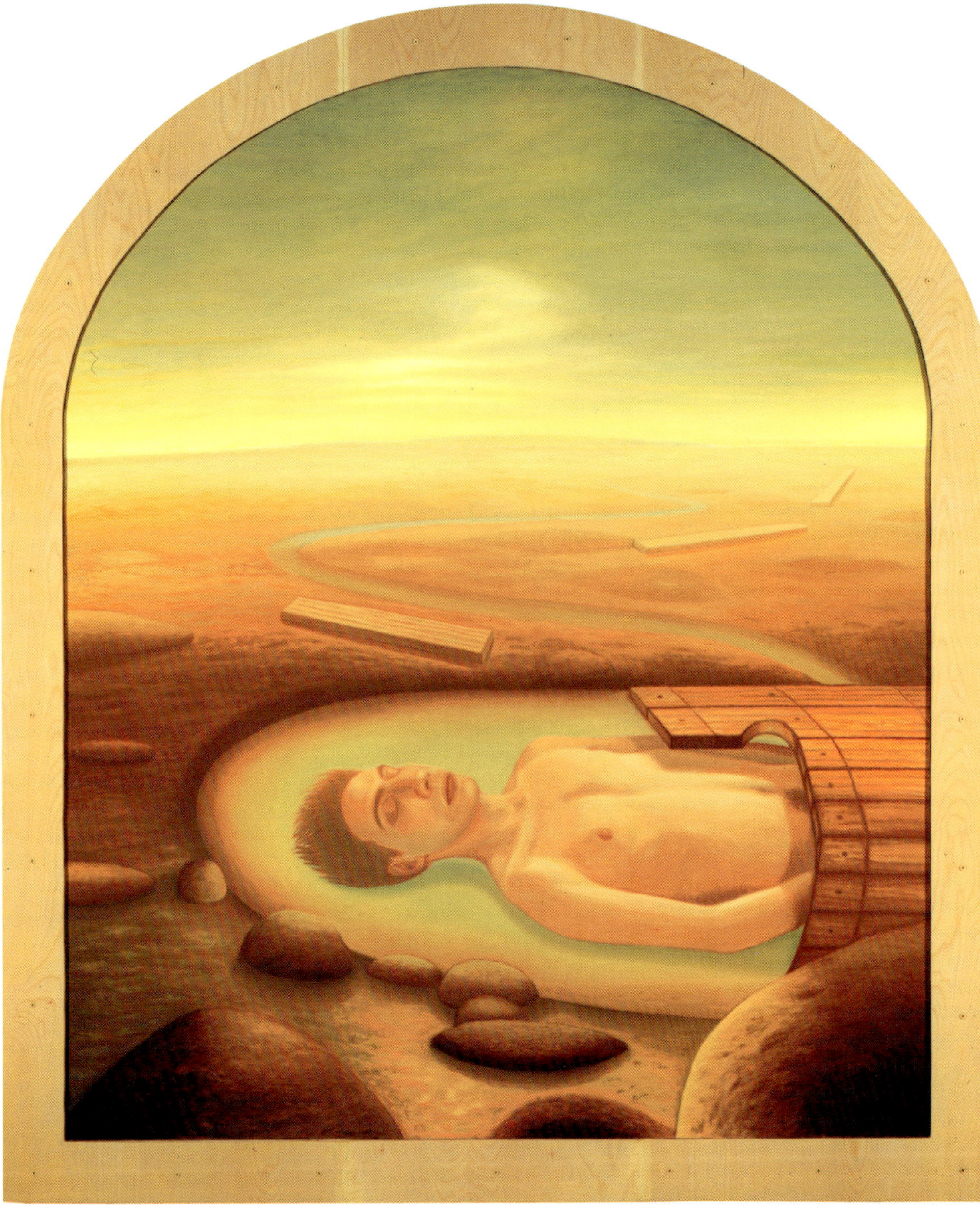

Floating Man 2 1990
oil on wood 83 x 68½ inches
Collection of The Detroit Institute of Arts

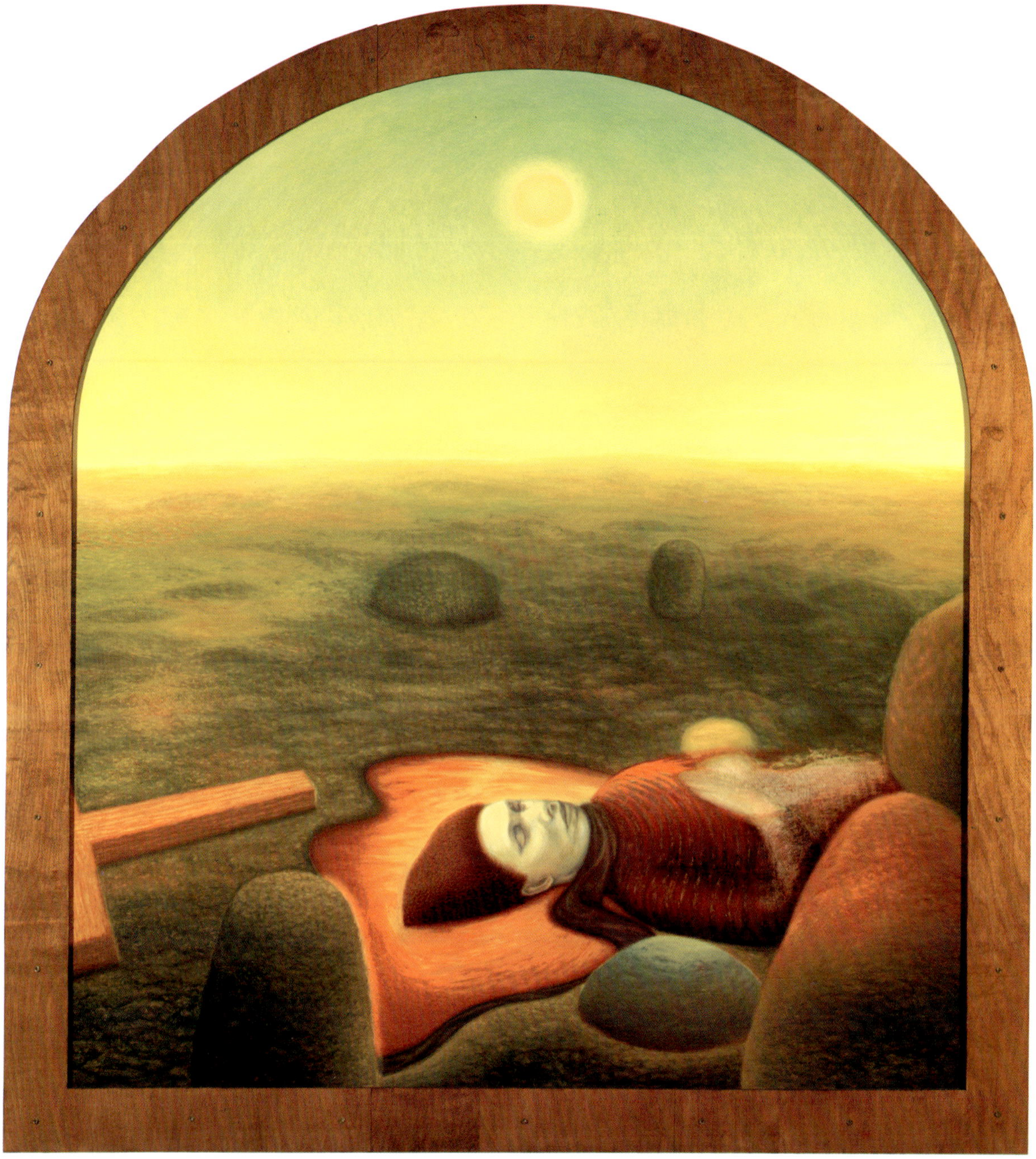

Eniskuo 1989
oil on wood 76 x 68 inches
Collection of Roberta Lindeman and Jim Meredith, Farmington Hills, MI

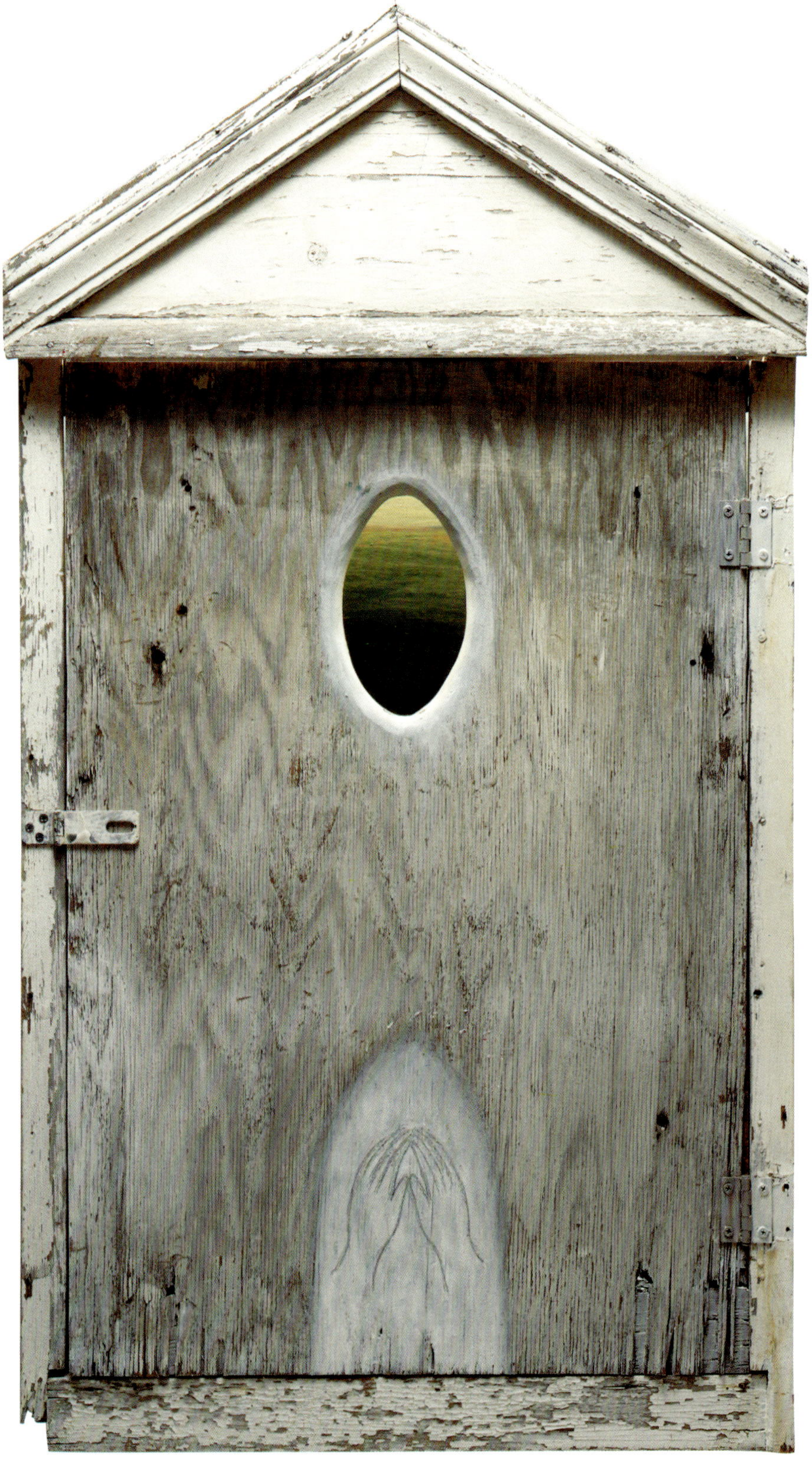

Leading the way to the Kingdom Eternal 1989
oil on wood, electric light, tabernacle door 45 x 24 x 4 inches
Collection of Elizabeth DuMouchelle, Bloomfield Hills, MI

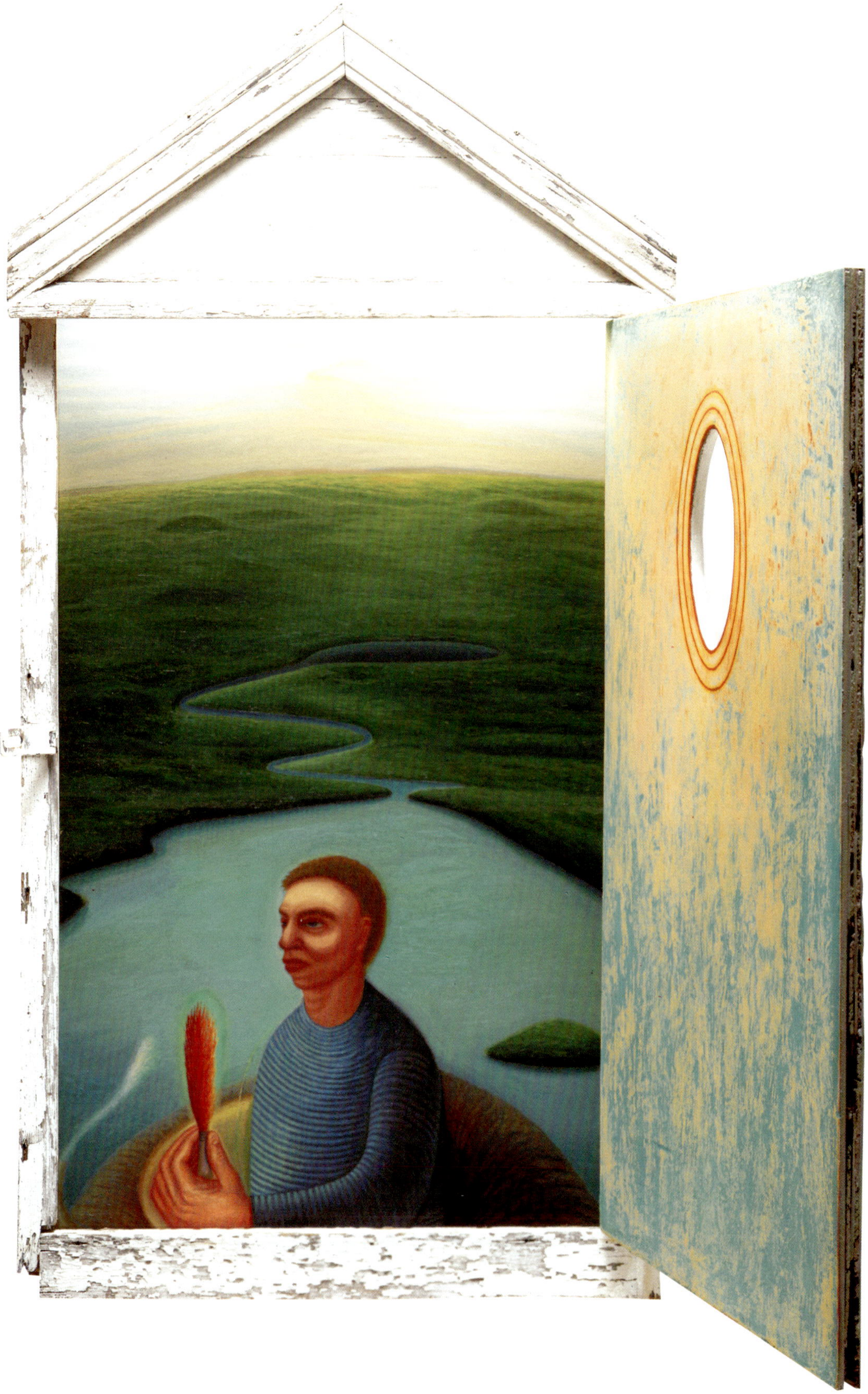

REQUIEM

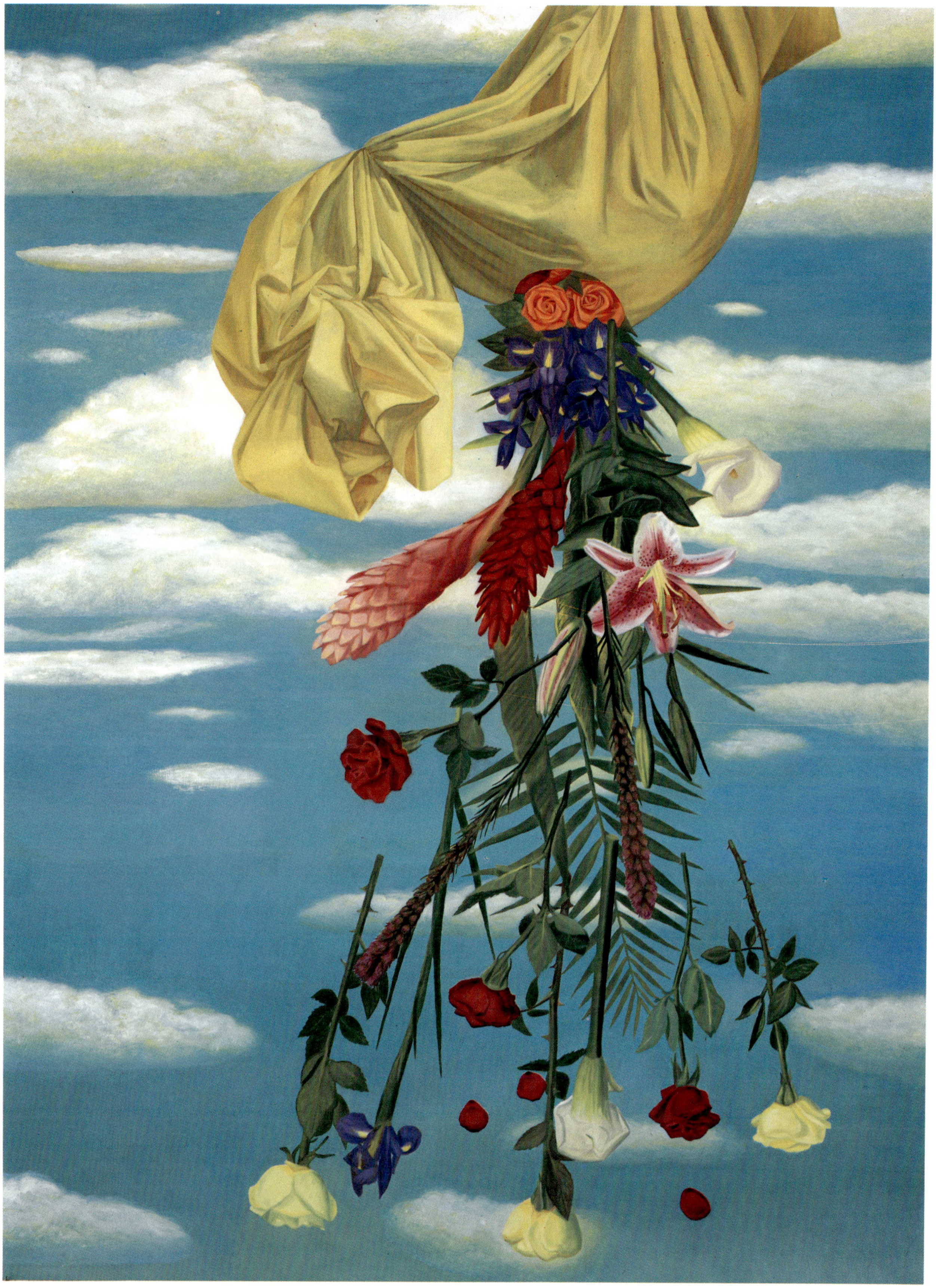

The Flight of Icarus 1993
oil on wood 78 x 60 inches
Collection of Lisa and Robert Katzman, Bloomfield Hills, MI

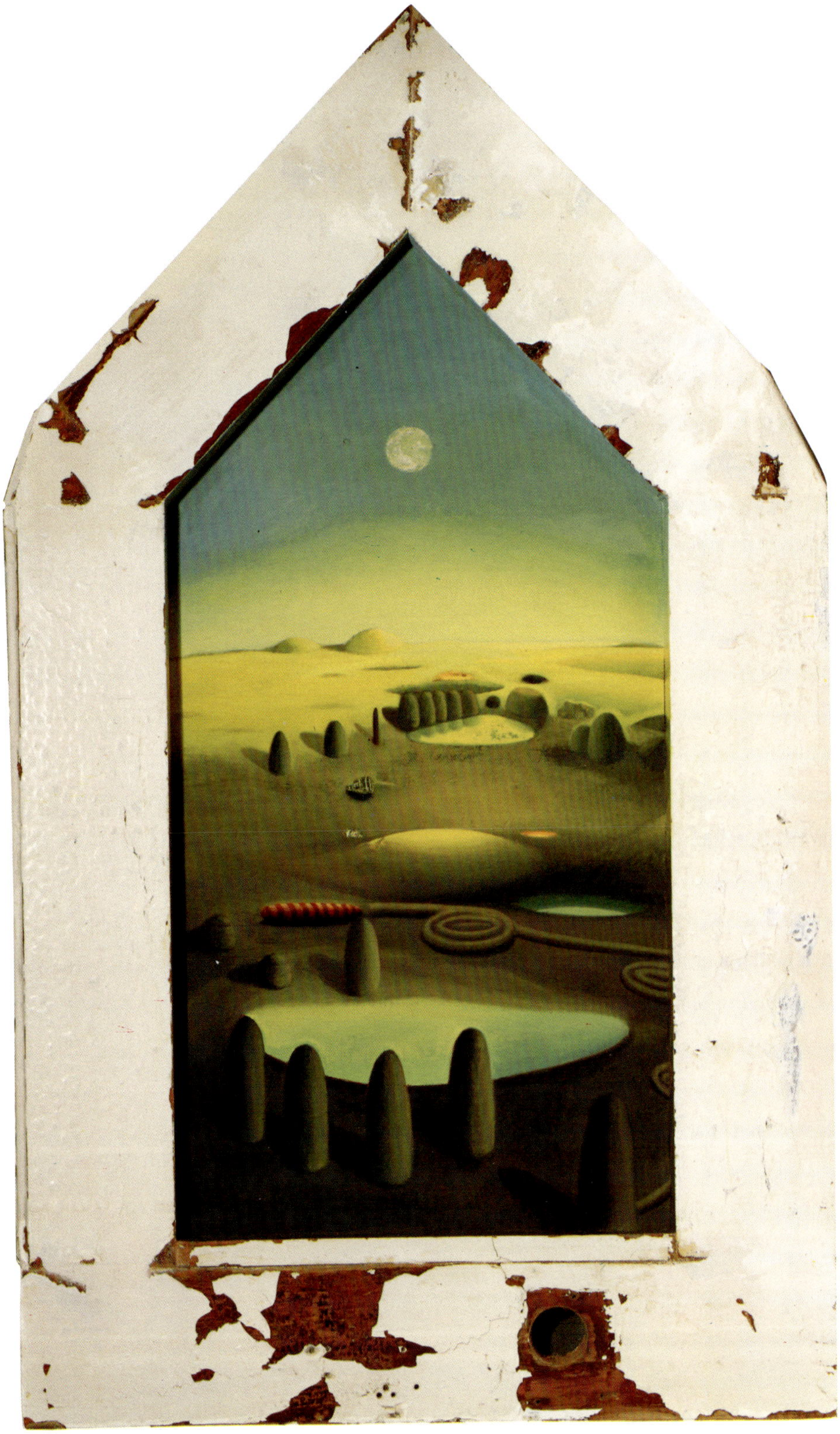

Burial Site 1992
oil on wood 37 x 21½ x 2½ inches
Private Collection

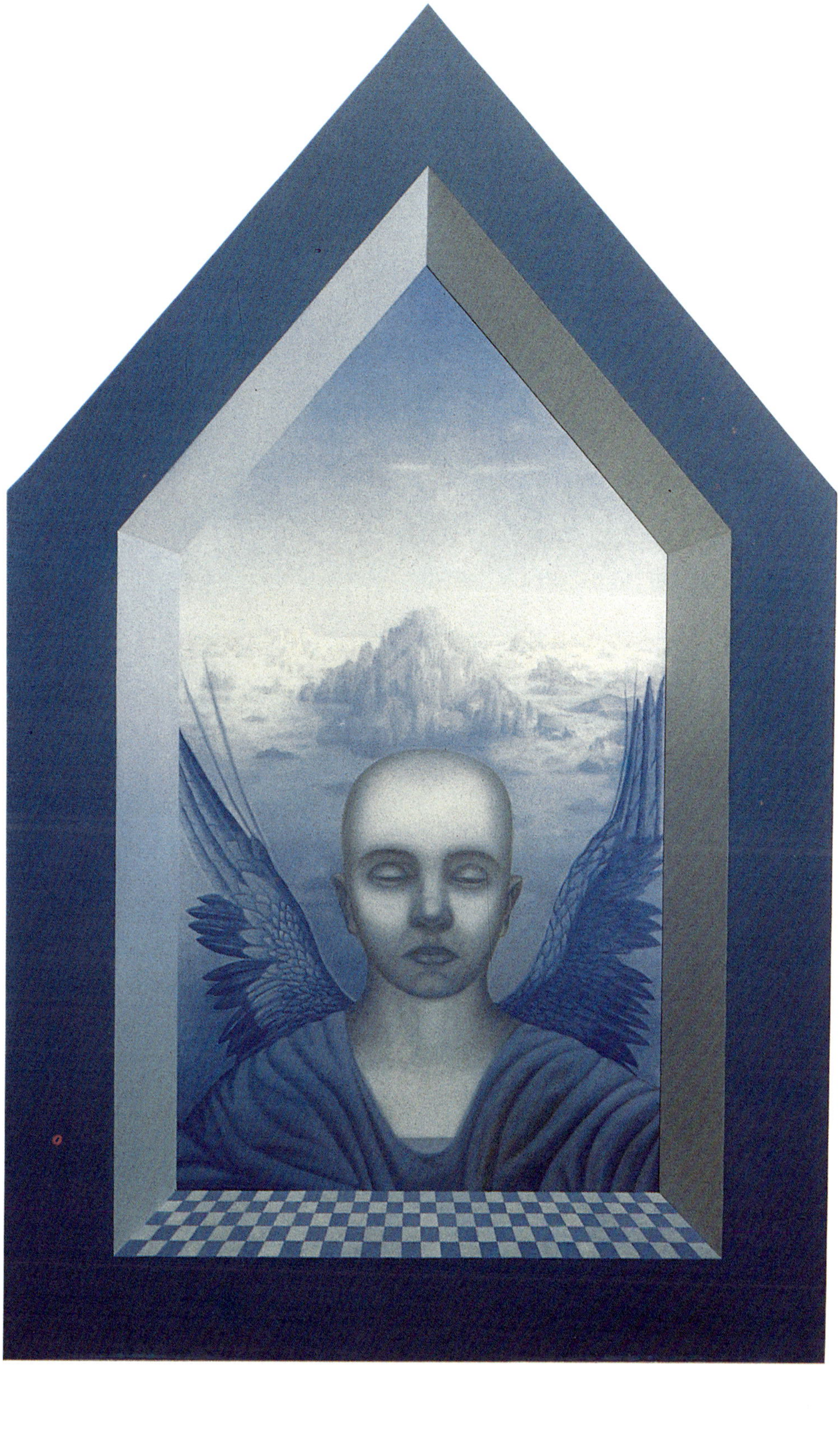

Blue Angel[3] 1994
oil on wood 36 x 52 x 3 inches
Collection of Cranbrook Art Museum, Bloomfield Hills, MI

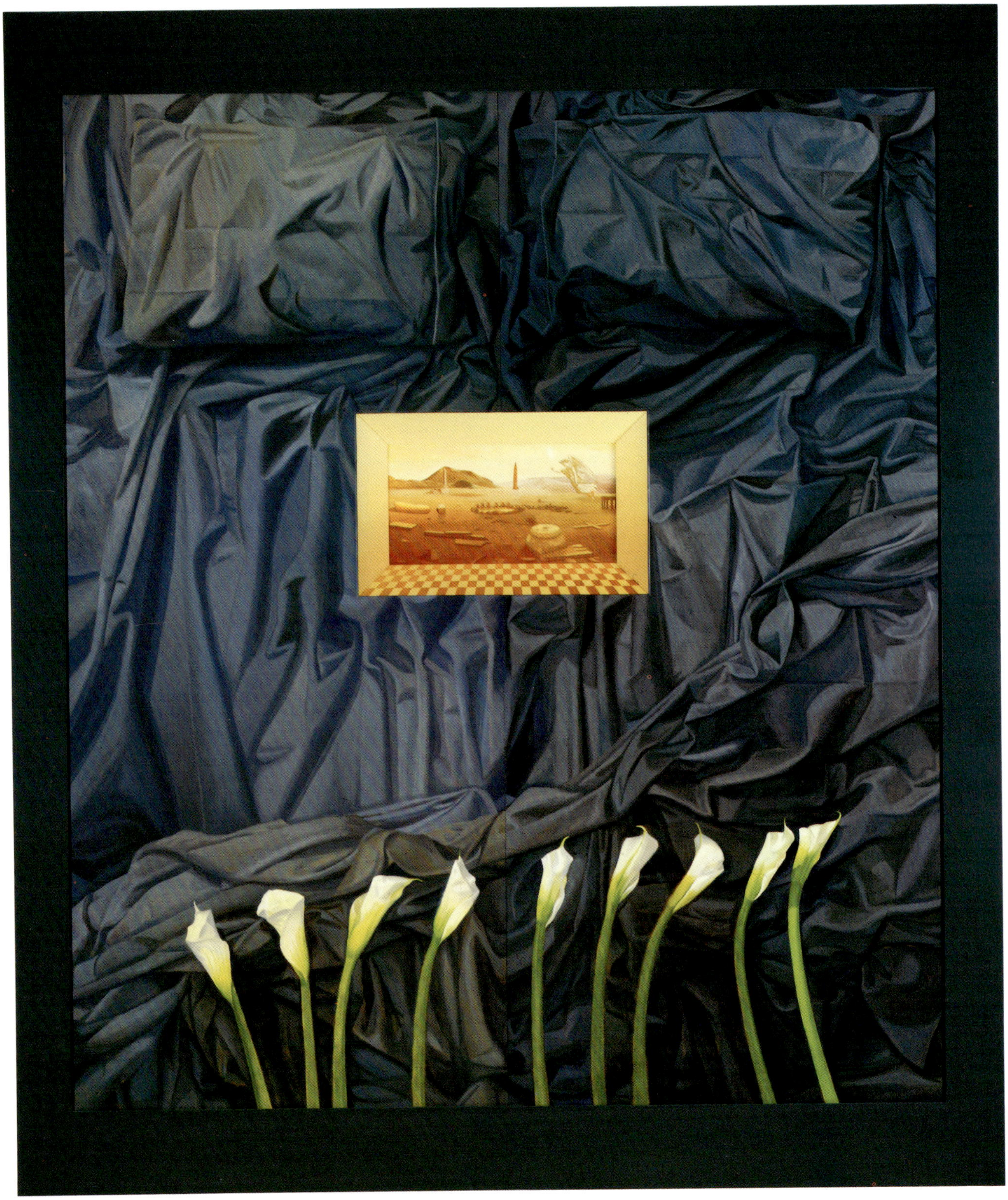

La Santa E Gloriosa Carne [4] 1994
oil on wood 84 x 72 x 4 inches
Collection of The Detroit Institute of Arts

His soul had approached that region where dwell the vast hosts of the dead. He was conscious of, but could not apprehend, their wayward and flickering existence. His own identity was fading out into a grey impalpable world: the solid world itself which these dead had one time reared and lived in was dissolving and dwindling.

The Dead, James Joyce

Solo Exhibitions

2001 *A Moment of Grace: A Retrospective of Ed Fraga,* Meadow Brook Art Gallery, Oakland University, Rochester, MI
2000 *All the World's a Stage,* Saginaw Art Museum, Saginaw, MI
1999 *In the Garden,* Lemberg Gallery, Birmingham, MI
1998 *A Selection of Small Paintings,* Mott Community College, Flint, MI
1996 *Dreaming of Suburbia and Other Places,* Lemberg Gallery, Birmingham,MI
1994 *The Isenheim Interior; An Installation,* Cranbrook Art Museum, Bloomfield Hills, MI
Side by Side; Lost Lives, Kalamazoo Institute of Arts, Kalamazoo, MI
1993 *Side by Side; Lost Lives,* Chicago Cultural Center, Chicago, IL
1992 *Sacred Places; Paintings,* Hill gallery, Birmingham, MI
1991 *Selections from the Eye Series,* Heike Pickett Gallery, Lexington, KY
1990 *Momentary Awakening,* Joy Emery Gallery, Grosse Pointe, MI
1986 *New Work,* Feigenson Gallery, Detroit, MI
1984 *Recent Constructions,* Feigenson Gallery, Detroit, MI
1982 *Drawings,* Michigan Gallery, Detroit, MI

Selected Group Exhibitions

2001 *The Art of the Catharctic Circle,* Meadow brook Art Gallery, Rochester, MI
2001 *New American Talent 15,* three locations: Del Rio Council for the Arts, Del Rio, TX; Buddy Holly Center, Lubbock, TX; Texarkana Regional Arts and Humanities Council, Texarkana, TX
2000 *New American Talent 15,* two locations: Shore Art Gallery Abilene Christian University, Abilene, TX; The Jones Center for Contemporary Art, Austin, TX
1999 *L'Avventura Artistica: Artists Under the Italian Influence: The Last Judgment; An Installation,* Ann Arbor Art Center, Ann Arbor, MI
1998 *A Sustaining Passion: The Tsagaris/Hilberry Collection,* Cedar Rapids Museum of Art, Cedar Rapids, IA
1997 *Scene/Unseen, Annual 1997,* Eastern New Mexico University, Portales, NM
1995 *Interventions,* Detroit Institute of Arts, Detroit, MI
1994 *The AIDS Cure Project,* King Plow Arts Center, Atlanta, GA
1993 *Haunting Images: Painting of Reference and Metaphor,* Foster Gallery, University of Wisconsin-Eau Claire, WI
Visceral Landscapes, Carl Hammer Gallery, Chicago, IL
1992 *Introducing,* Gwenda Jay Gallery, Chicago, IL
'92 Invitational, J. Cacciola Gallery, New York, NY
Expressive Visions, Exquisite Images, Meadow Brook Art Gallery, Oakland University, Rochester, MI
1991 *En el Corazon del Pais, Contemporary Latin Artists from the Midwest,* Chicago Public Library, Chicago, IL
1990 *The Book as Art/The Book in Art,* Barbara Fendrick Gallery, New York, NY
Awards in the Visual Arts 8, two locations: The BMW Gallery, New York, NY; Henry Art Gallery, University of Washington, Seattle, WA
1989 *Awards in the Visual Arts 8,* two locations: La Jolla Museum of Contemporary Art, La Jolla, CA; The High Museum of Art, Atlanta, GA
Eye for Art, Detroit Institute of Arts, Detroit, MI
Small Works, Fendrick Gallery, Washington, D.C.
1985 *Five from Detroit-The Figure,* Lebel Gallery, University of Windsor, Ontario, Canada
1979 *Italy '79,* Accademia, Venice, Italy

Education

1980 Wayne State University, Detroit, MI, BFA

Grants and Awards

1999 Art Serve Michigan, Creative Artist Grant
1995 Bellagio Center Residency, The Rockefeller Foundation
1993 Arts Foundation of Michigan
1992 Arts Midwest National Endowment for the Arts, Regional Visual Arts Fellowship Award
1989 Awards in the Visual Arts 8, N.E.A., B.M.W. of North America
Michigan Council for the Arts
1985 Michigan Council for the Arts

Selected Bibliography

2001 *An Eccentric Circle*, Frank Provenzano, Detroit Free Press, Mar. 6
2001 *The Art of the Catharctic Circle*, catalogue with an essay by Dick Goody, Director, Meadow Brook Art Gallery, Oakland University
2000 *New American Talent 15*, catalogue with an essay by David Pagel, curator and art critic, Los Angeles, CA
Art Museum Opens Ed Fraga Show, The Saginaw News, Sep. 2,
1999 Woodward Magazine, Oct. 1
A Leap of Faith, Frank Provenzano, Observer and Eccentric, Mar. 21
1997 Roger Green, Ann Arbor News, Aug. 31
Scene/Unseen, catalogue with an essay by Lucy Lippard, art critic and author
1996 *Ed Fraga's Small Pictures Look Right At Home,* Joy Hakanson Colby, Detroit News, Nov. 14
1994 *The Isenheim Interior; An Installation by Ed Fraga,* catalogue with an essay by David Rau, Associate Curator, Cranbrook Academy of Art Museum
The AIDS Cure Project Art Show, catalogue
Detroit artist brings serene images of death to Cranbrook, Marsha Miro, Detroit Free Press, Sept. 30
Shocking Image Inspires '90s Message at Cranbrook, Joy Hakanson Colby, Detroit News, Oct. 7
Roger Green, Ann Arbor News, Oct. 16
Amy Sult, Kalamazoo Gazette, Jan. 30
1993 *Side by Side; Lost Lives, Paintings by Ed Fraga,* Bonita McLaughlin, The Reader, Chicago, IL, Dec. 10
Karen Halverson, Museums, New City, Chicago, IL, Nov.
1992 *The Facets of Fraga,* Veronica Pasfield, Detroit Monthly, Sept.
1991 Vincent Carducci, Artforum, May
1990 *Detroiter's bizarre works push anxiety into tranquility,* Marsha Miro, Detroit Free Press, Sept. 14
Ed Fraga Momentary Awakening, Joy Emery Gallery, Grosse Pointe, MI, catalogue with an essay by MaryAnn Wilkinson, curator of Modern Art, DIA
Thomas Patin, Awards in the Visual Arts 8, Artspace
1989 *Awards in the Visual Arts 8,* catalogue with an essay by Jane Addams Allen, art critic, Washington Times and New Art Examiner
Amy Jinker-Lloyd, ARTS Magazine, Oct
Robert Pincus, San Diego Union, Sept. 3
William Wilson, L.A. Times, Aug. 27
Virginia Warren Smith, Atlanta Journal-Constitution, May 24
1987 *Proud Legacy,* Marsha Miro, Feigenson Gallery: Detroit Free Press, Dec. 13
1984 John Baron, Contemporary Relics, Monthly Detroit, June
Meg Cox, Wall Street Journal, May 22
Marsha Miro, Detroit Free Press, Feb. 10
Hope Palmer, New Art Examiner, April
1982 Dennis Alan Nawrocki, New Art Examiner, Summer

Public Collections

BMW of North America
Dow Chemical Company
Cranbrook Art Museum
Kalamazoo Institute of Arts
The Detroit Institute of Arts
Wayne State University

ACKNOWLEDGEMENTS

I wish to acknowledge with gratitude the names of several individuals who have supported my art over the years.

Jackie Feigenson gave dignity and respect for the art of Detroit. Her gallery in the Fisher building during the 70's and early 80's presented art in a professional space comparable to the finest New York galleries. Her gallery attracted serious collectors who bought much of the art she exhibited. I remember her saying, "I only show art that I would want to live with". My first show in her gallery sold out.

Sergio De Giusti continues to see the art that is produced in Detroit as a positive force for the city and its inhabitants. He gave me my first show at the Michigan Gallery and to this day values my evolving aesthetic.

Tim Thayer has been photographing my paintings since 1985. He is truly an "art lover." He is an expert in lighting and capturing the richness of each painting.

I am especially grateful to Dick Goody and Meadow Brook Art Gallery for hosting this exhibition and to all the private collectors who have lent their work.

Ed Fraga

MEADOW BROOK ART GALLERY

Department of Art and Art History
College of Arts and Sciences,
Oakland University

208 Wilson Hall, Oakland University, Rochester, MI 48309-4401
Tel (248) 370 - 3005, www.oakland.edu/mbag
ISBN 0-925859-11-7

1 *Aisreal* (Slavic); trans: angel who watches over the souls of the dead

2 *Floating Man,* 1990
Founders Society Purchase, Chaim, Fanny, Louis, Benjamin, Anne and Florence Kaufman Memorial Trust (DIA 1990.301)

3 *Blue Angel,* 1994
Collection of Cranbrook Art Museum, Gift of the Artist with additional funds from the Imerman Acquisition Fund (CAM 1995.7)

4 *La Santa E Gloriosa Carne,* 1993
Founders Society Purchase with funds from the Stroh Foundation, Andrew L. and Gayle Shaw Camden Contemporary and Decorative Arts Fund, and funds from Mr. and Mrs. Stanley R. Day, John Stroh III, Vivian W. Day, Martha Katz, Joy Emery, and Elizabeth DuMouchelle

cover image(detail): *The Visitation of Elizabeth and Mary* 2001 oil on wood 32½ x 21½ x 4 inches

Catalogue printed by Brophy, Detroit, MI